Groundcovers for the South

Marie Harrison

Pineapple Press, Inc.
Sarasota, Florida

Inquiries should be addressed to:

Pineapple Press, Inc.
P.O. Box 3889
Sarasota, Florida 34230

www.pineapplepress.com

Library of Congress Cataloging-in-Publication Data

Harrison, Marie, 1942-
    Groundcovers for the South / Marie Harrison.— 1st ed.
        p. cm.
    Includes bibliographical references and index.
    ISBN-13: 978-1-56164-347-9 (pbk. : alk. paper)
    ISBN-10: 1-56164-347-5 (pbk. : alk. paper)
    1.   Ground cover plants—Southern States.   I. Title.
    SB432.H37 2006
    635.9′64′0975—dc22

                                                              2005025317

First Edition
10 9 8 7 6 5 4 3 2 1

Design by Shé Heaton
Printed in China

Contents

Acknowledgments

Thanks to:

- Vivian Justice for her persistence in teaching me the fine points of English grammar and trying to make sure that they are incorporated in my books

- Editors and staff at Pineapple Press who make the finished product shine

- Amiable Spouse for his tolerance and patience

- Family and friends who continue to be supportive of my efforts

Hosta

Introduction

What is a groundcover?

Groundcovers, as their name indicates, are plants that cover the ground. They range in height from tiny one- or two-inch ground-hugging plants to shrubs, ferns, and other plants which grow much taller. Groundcovers can be woody or herbaceous, clumping or running, evergreen or deciduous, blooming or non-blooming, and can have needle-like or broad leaves. Actually, they can be any plants that are used to cover the ground in an area of the landscape.

A conventional lawn is the most common groundcover. Few surfaces are as ideal for children's play. Grass around the entry keeps sand from being tracked into the home. Toxins are removed from water as it percolates through the grass. Air is purified and temperatures moderated. The lawn is an important design element in most landscapes, and it adds a feeling of spaciousness to an area.

Many homeowners strive for the perfect lawn. When some folks drive down a street and look at other people's landscapes, they think that if the front lawn looks good, everything else on the premises is in order, both inside and outside the house. Some residents have been thought of as morally derelict and downright un-American if their lawns were not the traditional wide sweep of perfectly mowed and edged green grass.

Not that I'm in favor of unkempt landscapes. I appreciate neatness and neighborliness as much as the next person, but I am learning that having a neat landscape does not necessarily mean having fence-to-fence lawn. Trees, shrubs, and plants that offer habitat for wildlife and comfort for humans seem more desirable than endless lawn.

If a lawn is well-kept, it is the most labor-intensive area of the landscape. Regular mowing, fertilizing, watering, weeding, and edging are necessary to keep it neat and healthy. To some people, it's worth the effort. I'm ready to lighten up a bit.

Purposes and Uses of Groundcovers

Groundcovers add beauty and interest to the landscape. Attractive foliage and colorful flowers are refreshing alternatives to broad stretches of lawn. They bring unity to the garden if broad sweeps of the same groundcover are used underneath plantings of varied shrubs and flowers. They blanket soil with dense cover, add variety to the landscape, and reduce maintenance by suppressing weeds. When planted on steep slopes, groundcovers prevent soil erosion. There is much less possibility of mower damage to trees if they are surrounded with a groundcover.

Groundcovers can be used to create landscape patterns such as broad, flowing curves or geometric shapes. They can define a space and offer a smooth transition between the lawn and taller plants. Sometimes they are used to soften hardscapes such as walks, steps, and driveways. Tall groundcovers do not invite foot traffic, so they can be used to direct traffic without creating a sight barrier.

Asiatic jasmine is one of the most commonly used groundcovers.

Like other plants, groundcovers can be used to create moods. Small-leaved, smooth-textured groundcovers used in broad, curved plantings convey a feeling of spaciousness. On the other hand, large, coarse-textured plants create a sense of closeness. In addition, groundcovers shade soil and keep it from drying out, and many require much less moisture and fewer nutrients than grass.

Groundcovers can be used in many places in the landscape. Shady areas under trees or next to buildings are prime candidates for a groundcover. Groundcovers are naturals as underplantings in shrub borders and beds. A suitable groundcover is a logical solution where tree roots grow close to the surface and prevent grass from growing. Sometimes very wet or very dry locations can be attractively planted with a groundcover that suits those conditions. Naturally, in places where grass won't grow or is too difficult to maintain, a groundcover can be used. Small groundcovers are attractive in very small, confined areas. Any place where mowing is difficult is a suitable place for a groundcover.

Selection

Choosing groundcovers requires the same attention to detail as any other type of plant. The mantra "right plant, right place" is as true for groundcovers as it is for trees and shrubs. Determine if the area you wish to plant with a groundcover is shaded, sunny, or a mixture of both. Then decide if the soil is moist, dry, well drained, alkaline, or acidic. As always, choose plants that can tolerate the temperature extremes that can be expected in your climate. Of course, you'll want to choose groundcovers that blend with the surrounding plants.

Beware of invasive plants when selecting a groundcover. Sometimes the

8

term *vigorous* refers to plants that can be extremely aggressive in their growth habits. These plants are highly successful at self propagating and have the ability to compete and crowd out other plants. A few such plants are crown vetch (*Coronilla varia*), Japanese honeysuckle (*Lonicera japonica*), Bishop's weed (*Aegopodium podograria*), and English ivy (*Hedera helix*).

Many invasive plants are foreign imports. Away from their natural pests and diseases, these otherwise well-behaved plants might become garden thugs. Generally inexpensive and readily available, these attractive groundcovers may escape the garden and cause damage to the environment. Loss of habitat and food sources for native wildlife could result from careless and thoughtless selections of groundcovers for your area.

Planting

Prepare soil as for any other permanent planting. Performance will be as good as the effort put into this initial step, and it often determines the success or failure of your efforts.

Begin by removing weeds and competing plants. This can be accomplished by hoeing, pulling, or digging out by hand to remove whole roots or rhizomes. Sometimes it may be easier to kill the existing plants completely with a post emergent systemic herbicide such as glyphosate (Roundup). If signs of regrowth are evident, spot spray as necessary for complete kill. Another option is to cover with newspapers or black plastic for at least two weeks to smother plants that are there.

Plant directly into dead sod if existing soil structure is desirable and it is not necessary to correct for poor drainage or other conditions. If the area is steeply sloping, disturb it as little as possible to minimize erosion. Avoid dis-

A narrow strip between a fence and a sidewalk is a good place for attractive groundcovers.

turbance to shrub and tree roots as much as possible by digging individual planting pockets. Plant in staggered rows, and mulch well over the entire area. On slopes, use netting such as jute to hold plants and mulch in place. Jute comes in four- to six-foot wide rolls that can be unrolled from the top of the hill and held in place with wire staples.

If the soil needs amendments, add them to the entire planting bed, except on steep slopes and underneath trees and shrubs. Organic materials, leaf mold, compost, and well-rotted manure improve drainage in clay soils and increase water-holding capacity of sandy soils. Eight to ten bushels of organic materials per 100 square feet incorporated into the bed may be necessary in very poor or heavy soils. Work soil to a depth of six to eight inches.

A soil test will indicate which nutrients need to be added and if the pH is within the range of adaptability for the plants you choose. For most groundcovers a pH range between 5 and 7 is appropriate. Raise the pH by adding lime and lower by adding sulfur according to soil test recommendations. Without a soil test, and if existing plants seem to be growing well, do not alter soil pH. Simply add fertilizer. A general rule is to use three pounds of a commercial fertilizer such as 5-10-5 per 100 square feet. Fertilizer can be mixed into the soil at the same time as other amendments.

Water plants before removing them from containers. Spread tangled roots and set plants in prepared holes about the same depth as they grew in containers. Gently firm soil around each plant and water thoroughly. Spacing depends on such factors as how quickly you want complete coverage and the mature size of the plants you have chosen. Some prostrate shrubs may need three or more feet between plants. A rule of thumb is to determine the mature size of the groundcover and to space plants accordingly.

Maintenance

Groundcovers are rarely maintenance free. Water regularly until the planting is well established and then during dry periods. An occasional thorough soaking is better than light, frequent applications.

Keeping a new planting weed free, especially in the beginning, is important. Removing weeds by hand with minimum disturbance to the soil may be necessary until plants fill in. Walk around weekly and remove weeds as they appear. Mulch helps by starving weeds and making removal easier. Another option is to use a pre-emergent herbicide to prevent seed germination. One such product is trifluralin (Preen). Sprinkle it over the soil immediately after planting.

The benefits of a good mulch should not be underestimated. A one- to two-inch layer of leaf mold, compost, or similar organic material will help your groundcover get off to a good start. Mulch conserves soil moisture and reduces weed growth. In addition it moderates soil temperatures, improves soil structure, water retention, and oxygen diffusion. It reduces splashing from rain or irrigation water, thereby reducing the spread of disease. Beyond all that, a mulch dresses up your garden, giving it a more finished look. It should be reapplied as necessary to maintain depth.

Mulching materials can be almost anything. Frequently used materials include wood chips, conifer bark products, hardwood bark, shredded leaves,

Pine needles that fall from the tall pines supply mulch that is an integral part of this landscape.

stone, and pine needles. Each has its own advantages and disadvantages.

Wood chips are readily available and often free. A local tree service with a chipper may have chipped up limbs and tree tops available for the asking. These chips make ideal mulch at little or no cost. However, they may lack uniformity, and they can lose their decorative appearance with time. They decompose rapidly and may need to be replaced each growing season.

Bark products are also very popular mulches. Although bark and wood chips are both wood by-products, there are some differences. Any mulch sold with "bark" in its name must be at least 85% bark of the named tree, according to the National Bark and Soil Producers Association. Wood chips, on the other hand, have to be only 70% of the named material. The primary considerations are that wood chips break down more quickly than bark products, are more susceptible to insect damage, and discolor more quickly. Bark products have greater uniformity and longevity.

Bark products are readily available, attractive, and resistant to compaction and blowing wind. Usually bark chips are by-products of milled hardwood or conifer logs. Chips are available in chunks, nuggets (decorative), granules, or shredded, and they make excellent mulch. Shredded bark chips are often used as a soil amendment.

Pine needles and leaves are frequently used. They are easy to apply and readily available. Pine needles, when used for a long time, lower soil pH, so they are great for use around acid-loving plants. Leaves can be raked and shredded, or they can be vacuumed and shredded by the lawn mower. Allowing them to partially rot before use will prevent them from forming a mat that could block water penetration.

Mineral mulches such as crushed stone, gravel, and volcanic rock are very persistent and do not harbor weed seeds or diseases. Most of them are not easily blown about. However, they are sometimes not the best choice. They can migrate down into soil over time, and they can become a missile when caught just right by a lawn mower blade. Limestone chips raise soil pH, so one should limit their use around acid-loving plants.

Landscape fabrics are usually not recommended. Most fabrics allow water and oxygen to penetrate and inhibit some weed growth, but over a period of time weeds penetrate the fabric and grow in the organic matter on top of the fabric. Removing fabric from an established groundcover is a difficult task, since pulling up the fabric will likely result in pulling up much of the groundcover. Another danger is that tree roots may grow along the soil surface just under the fabric. If the roots dry out, the tree will suffer.

Groundcovers, like other plants, need fertilizer. All-purpose fertilizer can be incorporated at the time of bed preparation and planting. Annual fertilization may or may not be necessary. Plant performance is the key to making this decision. Minimal growth, small yellowish-green leaves, premature leaf drop, or poor flowering may indicate that fertilizer is needed. If a groundcover is thriving and additional growth is not desired, don't fertilize. If fertilizer is needed, apply a complete fertilizer such as 5-10-10 at the rate of one pound per 100 square feet.

Pruning may sometimes be necessary to rejuvenate plantings and to encourage new growth. This can be accomplished by shearing with hedge shears to cut back vigorous groundcovers or by mowing at the highest setting of the lawn mower. Some plants may need edging to keep them in bounds.

At times problems may crop up that require action. In such cases, be certain that you have correctly identified the problem, and make adjustments as necessary. Sometimes a plant simply needs to be moved to a more favorable site. Maybe you missed on the "right plant, right place" part of the formula. If insects or diseases are persistent, other actions may be necessary. Either get rid of the disease- or insect-infested plants, or identify the problem and select a product that will control it. Choose the least toxic product and apply according to label directions.

With a little guidance and education, groundcovers can be chosen that are beautiful, tough, and very useful for the busy gardener. As this book explains, many are available. Some trial and error will help to discover which ones do best in your garden. If you choose well and avoid the ones that are invasive, your garden will be easier to maintain as well as enriched with more texture, color, and variety.

Many plants, such as Lantana, tolerate both drought and salt.

Explanation of Data Charts

For each plant, the scientific name and its pronunciation, the family to which it belongs, and its common names have been listed. In addition, the origin of each plant, the size it can be expected to reach at maturity, and the USDA zones in which it can be expected to grow are given. Cultural information such as light exposure (sun, shade, partial shade), water use zone, soil preferences, and salt tolerance are included to help gardeners select plants and place them properly in their landscapes.

Water conservation is a matter of utmost importance. Extension agents and university researchers encourage homeowners to group their plants so that the best use can be made of available water. Water use zones are rated as high, moderate, and low. Plants in a high water use zone require water on a regular basis, and should be grouped together in the landscape and placed in the most water-retentive places. Those with moderate water needs should be irrigated less frequently, and those with low water needs are able to survive on natural rainfall except during periods of severe drought.

Salt tolerance is an important consideration for people who live near bodies of salt water. Salt spray and salt-laden moist air are not the only factors that limit plant selection. As wells pump water until they become depleted, salt water may intrude. If salt-tolerant plants are not chosen for these landscapes, the plants are doomed from the very beginning. For each plant, I have indicated the degree of salt tolerance.

A plant's tolerance to salt is rated as high, moderate, slight, or none. A plant with high salt tolerance can be planted in directly exposed locations near the ocean or gulf. Plants with moderate salt tolerance should be planted in a place where they are protected by a building or planting of more salt-

13

resistant species. Those with slight salt tolerance should be planted in even more protected places, and those with no salt tolerance should be chosen for locations well inland. For some plants I could find no information about the degree of salt tolerance; in these instances I have simply said "unknown."

Of great concern to everyone are the exotic pest plants that grow in yards throughout the South. Groundcovers are some of the worst offenders. By their very nature, they are designed to spread and out-compete weeds and other plants. One does not have to look very far to find groundcovers that have escaped their boundaries and invaded nearby woods and native areas.

This book will help people to recognize groundcovers that may become landscape thugs and to avoid them in their landscapes. To this end, I have included pictures and information about some of the worst offenders. Methods of reproduction and dispersal, the manner in which each plant is an ecological threat, and management approaches that gardeners can use to control them in their landscapes are discussed.

What's in a Name?

For each plant in this book, the scientific name is given as well as common names by which it is known. Also given is each family name. Related genera are grouped into families. In modern botanical nomenclature the name of a plant family is formed from the name of a genus in the family plus the suffix "-aceae."

Usually two words are enough to identify a plant: genus and species. Together these two names make up a plant's scientific name, which is recognized throughout the world. The first word, genus, refers to a group of plants that are closely related. The second word in the binomial is the species name, or specific epithet. Both are necessary to identify a species (genus name + species name = scientific or species name). Scientific names are always italicized because they are treated as Latin words.

Frequently a plant is a cultivar (cultivated variety). A cultivar is one that is selected because it is significantly different from the rest of the species. Usually the cultivar name is an English word, so it is not italicized, but the first letter of each word is capitalized. The cultivar name is enclosed in single quotation marks.

Pronunciation of the scientific name is also given in this book. However, Latin pronunciations differ from language to language and even from person to person. I have tried to find the most commonly used pronunciation, or the one that occurred most frequently in my research. If you pronounce the scientific names differently, go with it and pay no mind if the pronunciation I have chosen is different from the one you think is right. My decisions about pronunciation are certainly not final, nor are these the only accepted pronunciations.

The way we write scientific names is far more important than how we say them. Only one scientific name can be assigned to a species, but it may have many common names. Common names are fine for everyday conversation, but when we write about a particular plant, we must know its scientific name. Only then can we be sure that we're speaking the same "plant language."

Sometimes a scientific name is changed due to new scientific findings. In these instances, the old name is considered a synonym. I have listed synonyms in many places because it takes a long time for new names to become incorporated into the literature. Gardeners may find the plants listed at nurseries and in catalogs by the new scientific name or by its synonym, or former name.

Is this blanket flower? Or is it Indian blanket or firewheel? The scientific name, *Gaillardia pulchella,* is needed to positively identify this native plant.

USDA Plant Hardiness Zone Map

Zone	Temperature
1	Below -50
2a	-45 to -50
2b	-40 to -45
3a	-35 to -40
3b	-30 to -35
4a	-25 to -30
4b	-20 to -25
5a	-15 to -20
5b	-10 to -15
6a	-5 to -10
6b	0 to -5
7a	5 to 0
7b	10 to 5
8a	15 to 10
8b	20 to 15
9a	25 to 20
9b	30 to 25
10a	35 to 30
10b	40 to 35
11	40 and Above

The U.S. Department of Agriculture's Cold Hardiness Zone Map was first published in 1960 and updated in 1990. It is based on average annual minimum temperatures recorded throughout North America. Use the map to determine which plants will survive in your garden because they can withstand the average minimum temperatures listed on the map.

Keep in mind, however, that the map is only a guide. Other factors, such as soil type and fertility, soil moisture and drainage, exposure to sun and wind, humidity, and many other factors influence a plant's success or failure in the garden. Often microclimates in an area allow plants to be grown beyond the hardiness range suggested by the map. Global warming may also be a factor which, in recent years, has allowed plants to be grown beyond the areas indicated.

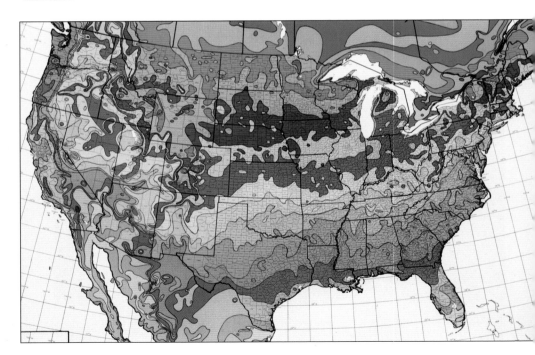

Chapter 1

An Array of Groundcovers

The author's landscape has served as a laboratory in which she
has grown and tried a wide array of groundcovers.

Lily of the Nile

Say: ag-uh-PANTH-us af-ri-KAHN-us
Family: Amaryllidaceae (Amaryllis)
Other names: African hyacinth,
    African lily, agapanthus
Origin: South Africa
Zones: 8–11
Light: Sun to partial shade

Water use zone: Moderate
Size: Up to 20 inches tall (foliage)
Soil: Organic, well-drained but mois-
    ture retentive
Salt tolerance: Moderate

Agapanthus has rhizomatous roots, strap-like leaves, and clusters of blue or white flowers (umbellate inflorescences) on stalks held above the leaves. It is an excellent groundcover plant for stabilizing soil on slopes and preventing erosion. Often it is selected for planting in difficult seaside gardens because of its salt tolerance and ability to stand up to the wind.

Right Place For best performance, give agapanthus rich, well-drained soil with plenty of decayed organic matter. It prefers full sun but will flower in partial shade.

Continued Care Lift and divide every four or five years to ensure flowering. Water deeply and thoroughly during the summer months. Remove old flowering stalks for a neat appearance. Although a light frost is tolerated, protection may be needed if the temperature drops below 20°F. Fertilize in spring with a slow-release fertilizer.

Propagation Division of established clumps is the best way to be sure that plants will be true to type. However, seeds can be sown fresh in late summer (or store them in the refrigerator until spring). Sow in trays in a mixture of sand and fine com-

post, and keep semi-shaded and moist. Seeds should germinate within six to eight weeks. Do not plant out until their second year, but pot up as necessary for good growth.

Kinds After much study and many changes, most botanists recognize six species of *Agapanthus.* Two are evergreen (*Aganpanthus africanus* and *A. praecox*), and four are deciduous (*A. campanulatus, A. caulescens, A. coddii,* and *A. inapertus*). However, confusion is rife in identifying the species. According to Scott Ogden in *Garden Bulbs of the South, Agapanthus africanus* seems to be the species that is the old, successful agapanthus of Southern gardens.

Other Uses Several medicinal properties have been attributed to agapanthus. Flowers are useful in cut flower arrangements, and they make excellent pot plants.

Ajuga

Say: uh-JOO-guh REP-tanz
Family: Lamiaceae (Mint)
Other names: Bugleweed, car-
petweed
Origin: Europe, Western Asia, Iran
Zones: 4–9

Light: Shade to partial shade
Water use zone: Moderate
Size: 6 to 9 inches in bloom
Soil: Acid to slightly acid, moist but
well drained, average fertility
Salt tolerance: Slight

Ajuga is an evergreen, spring-flowering perennial that forms a dense matlike groundcover. It spreads by underground stolons and tolerates a wide variety of soils and light conditions. Foliage may be light green or dark green, bronze, purple, or variegated, depending upon the cultivar. Mass plantings are excellent for erosion control because of the extensive root system. Many bees and butterflies are attracted when the plants are in bloom.

Right Place Shade or part shade is preferred, but considerable sun is tolerated. Soil should be moisture retentive, but it must be well-drained. A site that gets good air circulation is needed in hot, humid environments.

Continued Care Prune by mowing or cutting the foliage back to the ground after flowering. Thin out crowded masses to minimize crown rot. Consider installing a barrier to prevent creeping stolons from spreading to areas where they are not wanted. Moderate fertilizer may increase vigor and leaf size, but over-fertilization could stimulate succulent growth that is susceptible to rot.

Propagation Division of established clumps is the best way to be sure that plants will be true to type.

However, seeds can be sown fresh in late summer (or store them in the refrigerator until spring). Sow in trays in a mixture of sand and fine compost, and keep semi-shaded and moist. Seeds should germinate within six to eight weeks.

Kinds Several cultivars of ajuga are available. Some popular ones are 'Bronze Beauty', 'Burgundy Glow', 'Rubra', 'Pink Elf', 'Alba', 'Purple Brocade', 'Multicolor' or 'Rainbow', and 'Variegata'. Many of the variegated foliages will revert to their original color unless non-variegated foliage is periodically removed.

Other Uses Ajuga is very useful as a groundcover in areas that are too shady for grass to grow. It can be used in foundation plantings, beds, planters, or any place where its assets can be put to use.

Aloe saponaria
Soap Aloe

Say: AL-oh sap-oh-NAIR-ee-uh
Family: Liliaceae (Lily)
Other names: African aloe, zebra aloe
Origin: South Africa
Zones: 8B–11
Light: Sun to partial shade

Water use zone: Low
Size: Rosettes of leaves 1 to 1.5 feet tall and wide; flowers on stems to 3 feet
Soil: Sandy or gravelly with good drainage
Salt tolerance: High

Soap aloe forms a stemless rosette of foliage which hugs the ground. Pale green, lance-shaped, thick succulent leaves with white speckles are edged with sharp brown teeth. Showy yellow, orange, or red tubular flowers bloom during the summer on branched stalks held well above the foliage.

Excellent salt tolerance makes this aloe a good choice for seaside gardens. Drought tolerance allows it to be used in cactus or rock gardens. Avoid placing in areas where children play or near walkways—stems are armed and dangerous.

Right Place Plant soap aloe in sandy, well-drained soil in full sun to partial shade. Although bloom is best in full sun, the plants look better if some protection from hot afternoon sun is provided.

Continued Care Divide clumps as they become crowded. Protect from hard freezes. Although soap aloe can exist on natural rainfall, extra water during dry periods will keep the leaves attractive and plump. Remove old flower stalks after flowering is over. Fertilize once during the growing season with a light sprinkling of balanced fertilizer.

Propagation Get additional plants by separating the small plants, or pups, from the outside edges of the main rosette. Fresh seeds also germinate quickly.

Kinds About 300 species of aloe exist, and many of them are confused with members of the Agave family. Agaves have fibrous leaves, while aloes have juicy, non-fibrous leaves. Synonyms for soap aloe are *A. latifolia* and *A. maculata*. A variegated form is available in the trade. *Aloe vera (A. barbadensis)* is the medicinal aloe that is grown for its healing and soothing properties.

Other Uses Soap aloe grows well in containers. Very little soil is needed for it to thrive. Hummingbirds are attracted to the brightly colored, tubular flowers. Sap lathers up in water and can be used as a soap substitute. Use with caution, however, for the sap is an irritant to some people.

Aptenia cordifolia
Baby Sun Rose

Say: ap-TEE-nee-uh kor-dih-
  FOLE-ee-uh
Family: Aizoaceae (Fig-marigold)
Other names: Aptenia, Ice Plant
Origin: South Africa
Zones: 8B–11
Light: Sun

Water use zone: Moderate to low
Size: 3 to 4 inches by 3 feet
  (spreading)
Soil: Sandy, well-drained
Salt tolerance: High

Aptenia is a popular groundcover for hot, sunny places. Inch-long, succulent leaves provide the perfect backdrop for the small yellow to gold flowers that appear throughout the summer.

Plants are reputedly hardy to about 24°F. Cold weather kills them down to the ground, but they rebound with the onset of warm weather. North of Zone 8B, baby sun rose must be grown as an annual.

Right Place Choose a sunny place and well-drained, sandy soil. To establish a groundcover over a large area, plant individual plants 24 to 36 inches apart. Fertilize very lightly, and water when soil becomes dry. Roots can rot and the plants will die if soil is kept too moist.

Continued Care Trim or cut around the edges if plants grow out of bounds. Mulching during the winter may help it to come back in areas where it is marginally hardy. Fertilize very lightly in early spring, and water only when plants are thoroughly dry.

Propagation Baby sun rose is easily propagated from stem-tip cuttings. When stuck in moist soil, they root within two or three weeks. Rooting medium should be well-drained, or cuttings will rot. In six weeks they are actively growing and ready to be

planted in other areas of the landscape.

Kinds Confusion exists among the experts concerning the identification of baby sun rose. Most references indicate that *Aptenia cordifolia* is available in red or pink, and that a white sport is also available (a sport is a mutation, a genetic deviation that occurs naturally). Some references use the common name of ice plant, but that appellation is usually assigned to the *Delosperma* and *Lampranthus* genera. Yellow sun rose is also sometimes listed as *Platythyra haeckeliana*.

Other Uses Baby sun rose is a good choice for long-lasting hanging baskets or for cascading over the edges of planters and walls. Use it in rock gardens and other small, sunny spots where its fine texture and delicate appearance can be appreciated.

Arachis glabrata
Ornamental Peanut

Say: a-RAK-is GLAB-rah-tuh
Family: Fabaceae (Pea)
Other names: Perennial peanut
Origin: South America
Zones: 8B–11

Light: Sun to partial shade
Water use zone: Moderate to low
Size: 6 inches tall and spreading
Soil: Any well-drained, not acid
Salt tolerance: High

Ornamental peanut is a relative of the common peanut, *Arachis hypogaea*. Selections chosen for ornamental groundcovers reach about six inches high and produce yellow flowers throughout the summer. Tops will die back after frost, but plants will come back reliably if the rhizomes, which can grow several feet deep, are not frozen.

Perennial peanuts are well-suited to the hot climate and sandy soils found in parts of the South. Excellent results have been reported in the lower regions of southeastern states, extending from southeast Texas to southeast North Carolina.

Right Place Full sun is preferred, but ornamental peanuts can also grow in partial shade. They do not like acid soils, so a soil test may indicate a need to add lime. Well-drained soil is necessary. Add sand or organic matter to heavy clay soils to improve drainage.

Continued Care Once established, little or no maintenance is needed. Since peanuts are legumes, they fix their own nitrogen so little fertilizer is required. Height can be maintained at one and one-half inches tall if mowed every two to four weeks. Regular mowing also stimulates flowering. Weed control is important during the establishment period.

Propagation Division can be done after plants are well established. Since they spread by rhizomes, cutting off a few starts with roots will yield new plants. Tip cuttings can be made while plants are actively growing, and they can be added to the landscape as soon as roots are well established. New plants can also be started from seed.

Kinds Two cultivars, 'Arblick' and 'Ecoturf', are well-suited for use as low-maintenance groundcovers. Other cultivars such as 'Florigraze' and 'Arbrook' grow taller and are used mostly as forage crops.

Other Uses Use on berms or embankments where mowing is difficult or impossible. Peanuts can also be used as turf if they are mowed every two to four weeks.

Aspidistra elatior
Cast Iron Plant

Say: ass-pi-DISS-truh ee-LAY-tee-or
Family: Liliaceae (Lily)
Other names: Aspidistra, barroom plant, iron plant
Origin: Eastern Asia, China
Zones: 7–11
Light: Shade

Water use zone: Moderate to low
Size: 2 to 3 feet tall
Soil: Organic preferred, but also grows well in poor soil; must be well-drained
Salt tolerance: Moderate

Introduced into this country in 1824, aspidistra caught on quickly as a favorite in smoky barrooms and Victorian parlors. Today it remains a popular choice as gardeners take advantage of its cast iron constitution. Glossy dark-green leaves two to three feet long and six to eight inches wide adorn shady spots in many Southern gardens. Red flowers bloom at ground level and are seldom noticed.

Right Place Give aspidistra deep shade like that found under magnolias and giant live oaks. Amend soil with organic matter and maintain moisture until well established.

Continued Care Though drought-tolerant and able to survive with even the most abject neglect, aspidistra thrives when given moist soil and an occasional top-dressing of compost or balanced fertilizer. Once a year or so, remove old or tattered leaves.

Propagation Aspidistra is most easily propagated by division. Cut away a vigorous section of rhizome which has an actively growing tip, or dig an entire clump and separate it by pulling apart or cutting with a sharp knife.

Kinds The green-leafed *Aspidistra elatior* is most common, but the cultivar 'Variegata' or 'Okame' sports leaves with varied widths of green and white stripes. 'Asahi' has leaves that turn white in the upper third after it reaches maturity. 'Stars and Stripes' exhibits a combination of yellow-green stripes and white spots. 'Sei Ryu Ho' is a rare cultivar that has elongated yellowish spots and a brushing of white streaks at the top of the leaf. Other species of aspidistra also exist.

Other Uses Aspidistra has long been planted in containers and used as a porch or patio plant. It is also suitable for growing indoors. In shady areas it makes a great accent or edging plant, and it is a favorite of floral designers who bend, wire, twist, and cut it in a variety of ways.

Bletilla striata
Chinese Ground Orchid

Say: bleh-TILL-uh stry-AY-tuh
Family: Orchidaceae (Orchid)
Other names: Hyacinth orchid, hardy orchid, urn orchid
Origin: Japan, China
Zones: 5 (with protection)–9

Light: Shade (morning sun okay)
Water use zone: Moderate
Size: 8 to 18 inches tall and wide
Soil: Organic, well-drained, moisture retentive
Salt tolerance: Unknown

Right Place Chinese ground orchid prefers mostly shade, but morning sun is beneficial. Plant bulbs about four inches apart and a couple of inches deep in organically rich, well-drained soil. Mulch is beneficial and can be snuggled around the stems to help shelter the blossoms which sometimes bloom before the danger of frost is over. Fertilize just as growth begins in spring with balanced, slow-release fertilizer.

Continued Care Divide approximately every four years to promote flowering. Remove seed pods, and groom to remove unsightly foliage as needed. Best performance is in consistently moist soil.

Propagation Division of pseudobulbs is the method home gardeners use to propagate Chinese ground orchid. Fleshy tubers divide each year, so increase is steady.

Bletilla striata is most likely the only tuberous orchid that is easily grown by ordinary gardeners. Attractive long, thin leaves with longitudinal pleats cover the ground from early spring until frost and add an air of distinction to a shady area.

The most common form has rosy purple flowers, but a white-flowered variety is also available. Flowers look like tiny *Cattleya* blossoms and have five spreading petals and an undulating, furrowed lower lip.

Chinese ground orchids die down in winter and reappear in early spring. Although they are not evergreen, they hold their place in the garden for about three seasons.

Kinds The cultivar 'First Kiss' has white-edged leaves and white flowers with a flush of purple on the lip. 'Albo Striata' and 'Alba' have white flowers. *Bletilla ochracea* has yellow flowers.

Other Uses Chinese ground orchid is as attractive in pots and containers as it is in beds and borders. In Vietnam it has been used to treat tuberculosis and pulmonary diseases and to relieve pain from burns. An unidentified compound found in the plant promotes clotting of blood.

Bulbine frutescens
Bulbine

Say: BUL-bin-ee froo-TESS-enz
Family: Liliaceae (Lily)
Other names: Bulbinella, snake flower, cat's tail, burn jelly plant
Origin: South Africa
Zones: 8 (with protection)–11
Light: Sun preferred; tolerates some shade
Water use zone: Low
Size: 1 to 2 feet tall; 2 to 4 feet wide
Soil: Well-drained, tolerant of poor, dry soil
Salt tolerance: Unknown

Bulbine is a succulent, evergreen perennial groundcover. Fleshy green leaves similar to onion leaf blades arise from the base. Plants spread by rhizomes to create clumps. Small, six-petaled, star-shaped orange or yellow flowers with fluffy yellow stamens bloom on stalks held two or three feet above the foliage in spring through summer. Fruit is a small, rounded capsule containing black seeds which are easily dispersed by the wind.

Right Place Bulbine prefers full sun but can tolerate some shade. It requires well-drained soil and is tolerant of very poor, dry soil.

Continued Care Deadhead to promote flowering. Be careful not to overwater, especially in fall and winter. Although it can withstand light frost, a mulch offers some winter protection. Plants have low nutrient needs and are remarkably pest free.

Propagation Bulbine self-sows freely, so unwanted seedlings might appear. Transplant seedlings when they have four leaves and well-formed root systems. Starting new plants is easy—simply break off plantlets and pot them up until they are large enough to be planted in the garden. Division of clumps yields many new plants.

Kinds The cultivar 'Hallmark' is self-sterile, so seedlings will not be produced. It is smaller and more tidy than the species.

No other cultivars were uncovered during my research. Some references referred to the plant as *Bulbine fruticosa,* and *Bulbine caulescens* is a synonym, so it may be found under either of those names.

Other Uses Fresh leaves provide a jelly-like substance that can be used for treating burns, rashes, blisters, insect bites, and cracked skin. Bulbine is at home in the perennial garden, or it can be used as an accent plant, in containers, or in rock and cactus gardens.

Calathea louisae
Emerald Feather Calathea

Say: ka-lah-THEE-a (or ka-LAY-thee-uh) loo-EEZ-ie
Family: Marantaceae (Prayer plant)
Other names: Emerald feather, calathea
Origin: Tropical Americas
Zone: 8–11

Light: Shade to partial shade
Water use zone: Moderate
Size: 2 feet
Soil: Organic, well-drained
Salt Tolerance: Slight/none

Emerald feather calathea is an attractive, clump-forming perennial. It produces lance-shaped, dark green leaves that are purple to burgundy underneath. On the top, attractive silver brush strokes mark the center of each leaf. Leaves are oval, wavy along the edges, and up to one foot long held on stems that are about a foot long. Plants are root hardy in Zones 8 to 11, but frost will kill them to the ground. Each spring foliage returns to add a wonderful touch of color and texture to a shade garden. Grow in containers outside the hardiness range. In summer small flowers appear from spiky, light green bracts, but they are not particularly showy.

Right Place Calathea appreciates a place in the shade. Performance is best in organically rich soil, but it does well with far less. Mulch to maintain moisture and inhibit weed growth. Water regularly until established and fertilize to promote growth. Be sure soil is well drained. Plants have the greatest chance to succeed if they are able to dry thoroughly between waterings. Various fungi can attack wet leaves.

Continued Care Fertilize with slow-release fertilizer in spring just as growth begins. Remove winter-damaged fronds in early spring. Water during periods of drought. Gardeners who are tolerant of a few holes in the leaves will not find it necessary to treat for pests.

Propagation New plants are easy to obtain by dividing existing clumps. Simply dig a clump and separate it into individual plants or clumps with two or three plants. Replant in a prepared bed. If you grow these plants in containers, divide when crowded, or pot up to a larger container.

Kinds Many species of *Calathea* exist, but most are tropicals grown for their attractive foliage. Some, however, have striking flowers and are beautiful additions to tropical gardens.

Other Uses Emerald feather is popular as a container-grown plant which can be grown indoors in bright light.

Carex morrowii 'Variegata'
Variegated Japanese Sedge

Say: kar-eks mor-ROW-ee-eye
Family: Cyperaceae (Sedge)
Other names: Japanese sedge,
   Morrow's sedge
Origin: Japan
Zones: 5–9

Light: Partial shade
Water use zone: Moderate
Size: 10 to 12 inches and slowly
   clumping
Soil: Organic, well-drained
Salt tolerance: Slight

Japanese sedge is a pleasing addition to the landscape. Green leaves about 12 inches long fan out from a central crown and fall into graceful fountains. In most of the South, the plants are evergreen. Sedges are grasslike plants, but unlike grasses, they have triangular stems. Groups of four to six brownish, insignificant flowers bloom on spikes in spring.

Even though Japanese sedge is not really a grass, it is used like and resembles ornamental grasses in the landscape. It works especially well at the foreground of a partly shady bed. It serves as a foil for brightly colored plants and is an interesting contrast in texture with ferns and bold-leafed hostas.

Right Place Plant Japanese sedge in organically rich, well-drained soil that can be kept moist but where the foliage can dry out between waterings. For groundcover use, plant on 16-inch centers to allow some air space between plants. Protect from hot afternoon sun.

Continued Care Remove dead or damaged leaves in spring by combing through the plants with your gloved fingertips. Fertilize as growth begins with a general purpose, slow-release fertilizer. Sprinkle about a pint to 100 square feet of bed. Water regularly, as plants resent dry soil. Divide when clumps become too wide.

Propagation Japanese sedge is easily propagated by division of the clumps. Simply dig a clump and cut it into four or more sections. Replant the divisions in prepared garden soil.

Kinds *Carex morrowii* is one of many species of *Carex,* and 'Variegata' is one of several cultivars of *C. morrowii.* Other cultivars include 'Goldband', 'Fisher's Form', 'Silver Sceptre', and 'Ice Dance'. New introductions show up regularly, so keeping up with them could be a never-ending job.

Other Uses Use Japanese sedge to border beds or paths or in containers. It is one of the most effective plants that can be chosen to brighten up shady, dark corners in the landscape.

Ceratostigma plumbaginoides
Dwarf Plumbago

Say: ser-at-oh-STIG-ma
plum-bah-gi-NOI-deez
Family: Plumbaginaceae (Leadwort)
Other names: Leadwort, plumbago
Origin: China
Zones: 5–9
Light: Sun to partial shade

Water use zone: Moderate
Size: 6 to 10 inches by 18 to 24 inches
Soil: Well-drained, moist
Salt tolerance: Moderate

Dwarf plumbago is a deciduous (semi-evergreen in southern edge of its hardiness range) mat-forming perennial. It spreads by rhizomes to form an attractive groundcover six to ten inches tall. Shiny oval-shaped leaves about two inches long are green during the summer and turn bronze-red in fall. From summer through frost, attractive phloxlike blue flowers bloom in terminal clusters.

Plumbago deserves greater use in gardens across the South. It is a groundcover with multi-seasonal interest. On top of that, it attracts butterflies.

Right Place Dwarf plumbago grows well in a sunny to partially shady area, but best flowering is in full sun. Although it prefers fertile, moist, well-drained soil, it is tolerant of poor soil. Growth is more vigorous in rich soil.

Continued Care Prune winter damage just before new growth begins. Fertilize lightly as growth emerges in spring.

Propagation Lift and divide in spring just before new shoots appear. Do not attempt to divide in the fall, as the plant will probably die. New plants are easily started from tip cuttings inserted into moist soil. Pieces of underground runners can be removed and placed in a container or directly in the garden. Layering of new shoots is easy, and woody, old shoots can be layered if the bark is scraped or it is otherwise wounded before it is covered by soil.

Kinds *Ceratostigma plumbaginoides* may be listed under the synonym *C. larpentae.* Other species are *Plumbago auriculata* and *P. willmottianum,* which are both shrubs.

Other Uses Use dwarf plumbago as a border plant or in rock gardens, but carefully monitor its spread. Plant it underneath shrubs and it will stay on the ground and not climb up through the shrubs. Grow it in containers or let it spill over the edge of a wall. Overplant spring bulbs so that it will emerge to cover the unsightly bulb foliage as it dies.

Crinum erubescens
String Lily

Say: KRY-num er-yoo-BESS-enz
Family: Amaryllidaceae (Amaryllis)
Other names: None
Origin: South America
Zones: 7–10
Light: Partial shade

Water use zone: Moderate
Size: 1 to 3 feet tall and spreading
Soil: Organic, well-drained
Salt tolerance: Moderate

Tall flower stalks arise from the ground and hold milky-white, star-like flowers well above the foliage when the string lilies bloom. Beginning in July and continuing through the summer, the pinkish buds open to reveal large, fragrant flowers. Rosy stamens perch above the flowers, giving them an ethereal, spidery look. Strap-shaped leaves provide substance in the garden until frost.

Crinum erubescens closely resembles our native *C. ameri-canum.* As a matter of fact, the two look identical. Gardeners, however, will have no trouble deciding which one they have. *C. erubescens* grows well in ordinary garden soil. *Crinum americanum,* on the other hand, grows and blooms best on boggy or wet sites.

Right Place Plant this crinum in ordinary garden soil and give it some protection from harsh afternoon sun. Soil should be moderately fertile, but plants will grow too vigorously if the soil is too rich.

Continued Care Foliage is killed to the ground by a freeze, but it comes back up reliably in spring. Rhizomes run about quite freely in good garden soil, so division may be required. A boundary or structure may be needed to keep plants within bounds.

Propagation Getting additional plants is as easy as dividing the wide-ranging roots. Plants are easily dug and replanted where desired, or extras can be potted up to share.

Kinds Horticultural literature gives several different scientific names to *Crinum erubescens.* Some are *Crinum americanum* 'Robustum', *Crinum americanum* forma *erubescens,* and *C. americanum* var. *robustum.*

According to Scott Ogden's *Garden Bulbs for the South,* there is a miniature form of this crinum. It behaves much like the larger *C. erubescens,* but tiny flowers reach only about six inches tall. He suggests that this diminutive version would be useful as a small-scale groundcover.

Other Uses *C. erubescens* grows well in tubs and other containers. As a matter of fact, tub culture is sometimes recommended as a method to keep growth in bounds.

Cuphea hyssopifolia
Mexican Heather

Say: KYOO-fee-uh
   hiss-sop-ih-FOH-lee-uh
Family: Lythraceae (Loosestrife)
Other names: False heather, heather,
   Hawaiian heather, elfin herb
Origin: Mexico, Guatemala
Zones: 8B–11

Light: Sun to partial shade
Water use zone: Moderate to low
Size: 1 to 2 feet by 2 to 3 feet
Soil: Adaptable; loam, acidic, alka-
   line, clay, sand, well-drained
Salt tolerance: None

Mexican heather is a very popular landscape plant in the Deep South. Hundreds of white, pink, violet or reddish purple flowers appear in the axils of new leaves. Arching stems of finely textured leaflets reach out two or three feet on a low-growing, mannerly plant. Such characteristics make it ideal for a groundcover or border plant in many landscape situations.

Right Place Plant on two-foot centers for a quick covering groundcover in almost any soil type provided it is well drained. Place in full to partial sun, and water regularly until it is well established, after which it is very drought tolerant. Fertilize lightly but frequently and mulch thickly with an organic mulch. Grow as an annual in Zones 7 and below.

Continued Care Pinch growing tips to encourage bushiness and compact growth. Rejuvenate older plants in early spring or late winter with severe pruning or shearing. Plants may be killed to the ground in Zones 8 and 9 but will resprout from the base if well-mulched. Nematodes, mites, flea beetles, and occasional caterpillars may cause problems. Treat if necessary.

Propagation New plants can be started by layering, cuttings, or seeds. Although seeds are difficult to collect, they are produced abundantly. Collect and transplant seedlings as they sprout beneath existing plants. Large clumps can be divided. Also, cuttings four to six inches long taken from the tips root easily.

Kinds By some accounts there are as many as 260 species of *Cuphea*. Within the species *Cuphea hyssopifolia,* many cultivars exist. In addition, the species goes by several other names. Synonyms are *Parsonsia hyssopifolia, Cuphea carthaginensis, Parsonia petiolata,* and *Cuphia petiolata.*

Other Uses Mexican heather is an excellent plant for containers, low borders, parking lot islands, and as an edging plant. It attracts butterflies and bees. In tropical climates it could become weedy, so caution is advised. In parts of Hawaii it has become a serious weed problem.

Delosperma cooperi
Ice Plant

Say: del-oh-SPUR-muh KU-per-eye
Family: Aizoaceae (Fig-marigold)
Other names: Trailing ice plant,
    hardy ice plant
Origin: South Africa
Zones: 6–10
Light: Sun

Water use zone: Low
Size: 3 inches tall and spreading
Soil: Well-drained dry, sandy, or
    rocky
Salt tolerance: High

Right Place Plant hardy ice plant in full sun and in deep, well-drained, lean soil. For groundcover effect, place plants about twelve inches apart.

Continued Care Water only during periods of drought. Fertilize once early in the growing season with a light sprinkling of all-purpose fertilizer. The main enemy to vigorous growth is wet soil, especially during the winter months. Thin out during wet seasons to allow air circulation and the driest conditions possible. Although ice plant can take the heat of Southern summers, extended high humidity may lead to its demise.

Propagation *Delosperma* is easily started by cuttings. Individual leaves sprinkled on a prepared surface will root in a matter a few days.

Hardy ice plant was brought from South Africa to England by botanist and plant explorer Thomas Cooper in the mid to late 1800s. The popularity of this perennial evergreen succulent has not waned since its introduction.

Thick, somewhat cylindrical leaves are about two and one-fourth inches long and a quarter-inch wide. Two-inch, magenta, aster-like flowers cover the plants during sunny hours most of the summer. In fall, the fat leaves turn golden yellow and have a hint of pink at their tips.

The common name comes from bladder-like hairs on the leaf surfaces that reflect light and look like tiny ice crystals. Ice plant takes heat well and requires very little water to keep it growing vigorously.

Kinds Some other species of plants are called ice plants. One relative (*Carpobrotus edulis*) is an exotic invasive plant that is banned in some states. *Delosperma nubigenum* is similar in appearance but is more hardy than *D. cooperi*.

Other Uses Hardy ice plant can be grown in containers, rock gardens, or on slopes. Butterflies are attracted to the blossoms. Since it is fire resistant, it may be a good plant for drought-prone areas where fires are frequent.

Dietes vegeta
African Iris

Say: dee-ATE-ees veg-AH-tuh
Family: Iridaceae (Iris)
Other names: Fortnight lily, butterfly iris
Origin: Eastern Africa
Zones: 8–10
Light: Sun to partial shade

Water use zone: Moderate to low
Size: 4 feet by 2 feet (taller in wet soil or water)
Soil: Best on rich, moist soil, but tolerant of less than ideal soil
Salt tolerance: Slight to none

African iris is a clumping, evergreen perennial that is frequently used as a groundcover. Leaves radiate up and out in a fan-shaped pattern. Irislike flowers are white with yellow and blue markings. Although the three-inch flowers last only two days, they are produced throughout the year. Flowers are most abundant in spring and early summer.

Right Place Preference is for rich, moist soil. As a matter of fact, African iris is well adapted to water gardens. Interestingly, it is also tolerant of drought and grows satisfactorily on dry soil. It appreciates and blooms best in full sun but also does well in part shade. For groundcover use, place individual plants 24 to 36 inches apart. Nematodes may be problematic. They are best controlled by adding organic matter to the soil.

Continued Care Cold temperature can cause leaves to turn brown. These can be removed in spring. Fertilize lightly once or twice a year to increase growth rate and flower production. Divide every two or three years.

Propagation Lift plants and divide rhizomes every three years or when new plants are needed. Seeds can be planted in spring or fall. Protect seedlings during the winter for the first year, and then plant in permanent places in the landscape.

Kinds The cultivar 'Johnsonii' has larger leaves and flowers than the species. Plants may be sold by its synonyms: *Moraea vegeta, Dietes iridioides,* and *Moraea iridioides.*

A similar species is *Dietes bicolor.* Growing conditions are similar, but the leaf is narrower and the plant is finer textured than *Dietes vegeta.* Flowers are yellow and marked with black or orange.

Other Uses African iris is useful in mass plantings, containers, water gardens, and for growing indoors in containers. Use it as an accent plant in perennial beds where it adds a contrasting spiky form among lower-growing, broad-leafed perennials.

Evolvulus glomeratus
Blue Daze

Say: ee-VOLV-yoo-lus
 glom-mer-RAY-tus
Family: Convolvulaceae (Morning
 glory)
Other names: Evolvulus
Origin: Brazil, Paraguay

Zones: 9 (if well-mulched)–11
Light: Sun to partial shade
Water use zone: Low
Size: 6 to 12 inches by 2 to 3 feet
Soil: Well-drained
Salt tolerance: Moderate to high

Evolvulus is a nonvining member of the morning glory family. It is ideal to use massed as a ground-cover in areas where it is hardy. An evergreen subshrub, it eventually forms a gray-green carpetlike cover. The attractive, mounding plant sports feltlike, blue-green leaves that are about one inch long and half an inch wide. Blue, one-inch, funnel-shaped, white-centered flowers bloom profusely during the summer. Even though the flowers close by early afternoon, new ones open the following morning.

Right Place For groundcover use, plant on 20- to 24-inch centers in an area with good air circulation. Plant in a sunny area, and be sure that soil is well drained. Evolvulus cannot survive in consistently wet soil. Fungal diseases may occur if foliage remains wet for long periods of time.

Continued Care Protect from freezing temperatures, or grow as an annual. Very little fertilization is needed, and additional watering is not usually required once plants are established. Keep well mulched, especially in winter in areas where it is marginally hardy. There are no known pest problems.

Propagation Blue daze can be started from seed or softwood stem cuttings. Take softwood stem cuttings and stick them in well-drained, damp potting soil. Check underneath plants, because stems root where they touch the ground. These can easily be removed. Outside its hardiness range, new plants can be started in late summer and overwintered indoors in a cool, bright location.

Kinds The cultivars 'Blue Daze' and 'Hawaiian Blue Eyes' are commonly available. Sometimes *Evolvulus glomeratus* is confused with *Evolvulus pilosus* (syn. *E. nuttallianus*) which is a more hardy species native to Midwestern North America.

Other Uses Use blue daze in the border or as an edging plant. It is spectacular in containers and hanging baskets or cascading from planters. Salt tolerance makes it a good choice for seaside and coastal gardens.

Ficus pumila

Creeping Fig

Say: FYE-cus PEW-mil-luh
Family: Moraceae (Mulberry)
Other names: Climbing fig, creeping rubber plant
Origin: South China through Malaysia
Zones: 8–11

Light: Shade to partial shade
Water use zone: Moderate when young, low when mature
Size: To top of supporting structure
Soil: Not particular
Salt tolerance: High

Creeping fig is a vine that is commonly planted in warm climates as a cover on rock walls, trees, and other structures. A powerful adhesive enables it to scramble up vertical surfaces until it reaches the top. It creates a dense green covering of fine, attractive foliage, particularly in shady places.

Right Place Creeping fig grows almost anywhere, but full sun tends to cause the foliage to become yellow. Most attractive growth is in shade to partial shade, and its most frequent use is to provide a covering for vertical surfaces.

Continued Care Careful attention must be given to pruning if creeping fig is used as a groundcover and vertical growth is not desired. Regular pruning along the edges will keep it in bounds. It is capable of aggressive vegetative growth and can become a nuisance by climbing high into trees and growing beyond the desired area.

Propagation Creeping fig roots where it touches the ground, so layering is a good way to get new plants. They can also be started by taking cuttings, dusting the end with rooting hormone powder, and sticking in damp soil.

Kinds Cultivars include 'Minima', which has small, slender leaves; 'Quercifolia', which has tiny, oaklike leaves; and 'Variegata', which is shown in the picture. Two kinds of foliage appear on the plants. Juvenile foliage is fine and sticks closely to the surface. Once the vine reaches the top of its support, horizontal branches form and leathery adult leaves about three inches long by two inches wide begin growing. If left untrimmed, the vine turns into a woody shrublike plant.

Other Uses Curtains of cool green will grow to cover unattractive block, masonry, and concrete walls. It lends itself to quick topiary on wire frames formed into various shapes. In hanging baskets or container gardens, it quickly drapes over the edges. When used as a groundcover, it is attractive scrambling over rocks and other objects.

Hedera canariensis

Algerian Ivy

Say: HED-dur-uh kuh-nair-ee-EN-sis
Family: Araliaceae (Ginseng)
Other names: Canary Island ivy
Origin: Canary Islands, Portugal, the Azores, North Africa
Zones: 8B–10
Light: Shade to partial shade

Water use zone: Moderate
Size: To top and width of supporting structure
Soil: Best in rich, moist soil but not fussy about pH
Salt tolerance: High

Algerian Ivy is an evergreen, trailing vine that climbs by aerial roots. Moderate to rapid growth and large, attractive leaves make it useful as a coarse-textured groundcover that adds uniformity to the landscape. Leaves may turn bronze during the winter. Fruit is a fleshy, inconspicuous berry less than half an inch in diameter. Thick, glossy foliage and red leaf stems add to its attractiveness.

Right Place Although Algerian ivy is tolerant of sun, it is at its best when grown in shade. Moist, well-drained soil is preferred, but it is moderately drought tolerant once established. Grow in protected areas as it is subject to damage at temperatures below 20°F. Salt tolerance makes it useful for areas near bodies of salt water.

Continued Care Take care to direct growth where it is wanted and to contain the plants within the desired area. Regular pruning along the edges of beds will be required. Although usually not bothered by diseases, leaf spot can be a problem if plants are grown where there is little air circulation. Other problems may include scale, sooty mold, and snails, but long-term health is usually not affected by these pests. Fertilize lightly with balanced fertilizer in spring.

Propagation Cuttings of young shoots are best started in middle to late spring after active growth has begun. Layering is easily accomplished by covering growing shoots with soil.

Kinds Several cultivars are available. Some are solid green, and others sport variegated leaves. Look for such cultivars as 'Variegata', 'Canary Cream', 'Gloire de Marengo', 'Marginomaculata', 'Ravensholst', and 'Striata', among others.

Other Uses Algerian ivy can be grown as a houseplant, and it is very useful in hanging baskets or tumbling over the edges of containers or above-ground planters. It can be used to clamber over or to cover walls, fences, and trellises.

Say: hem-er-oh-KAL-iss
Family: Liliaceae (Lily)
Other names: None
Origin: China, Korea, Japan
Zones: 2–10
Light: Sun

Water use zone: Moderate
Size: 10 to 40 inches tall and clumping
Soil: Organic, well-drained
Salt tolerance: High

Right Place Full sun to partial shade in neutral, slightly acid, organic, well-drained soil suits daylilies well. They should be planted in a place where they will not have to compete with tree roots for water and nutrients, and they benefit from protection from hot afternoon sun in the Deep South.

Continued Care Although drought tolerant, daylilies perform much better with at least one inch of water a week. Fertilize as growth begins in spring and again just after the bloom cycle. Mulch, but avoid placing it near the crown. Divide clumps every three to five years for best growth and flowering.

Propagation Daylilies can be propagated by seed, but this is usually left to hobby gardeners or hybridizers. Most gardeners will have best results by dividing existing clumps or by

Flowers of the daylily last for one day only, but since several are on a scape, bloom may last for weeks. Daylilies may be evergreen, semi-evergreen, or dormant, and are classified as early, mid-season, or late-season bloomers and by flower height, size, color, and shape. They can be tetraploid or diploid, and all colors except true blue and pure white have been produced.

Once thought to be the most carefree of perennials, a new disease has cropped up that shatters that assumption. Daylily rust was found in the United States in 2000, and has since spread to at least 21 states. The disease is spread by airborne spores and through the movement of plants. See page 37 for further information and a list of disease-resistant varieties.

planting proliferations that occur on the scapes of some varieties.

Kinds Literally thousands of daylily cultivars are in existence, and new ones are registered yearly.

Other Uses Daylilies are widely planted in perennial beds and borders, and many are well-suited to container culture. Salt tolerance makes them ideal for use near bodies of salt water. They make an excellent groundcover when planted en masse.

Daylily Rust

Control of daylily rust requires a combination of sanitation, a regular application of approved fungicides, and selection of resistant varieties. (See the list below.)

Rust appears on the leaves as small, water-soaked spots. The spots expand and become raised pustules which release powdery spores that are easily transported by wind. Daylily rust spores are bright orange and are evident on both the upper and lower leaf surfaces. A good field test is to rub a leaf with a white facial tissue. If the rust is present on the leaves, an orange-yellow stain will come off on the tissue. The disease can be confused with other leaf problems, such as leaf streak disease. No orange stain will result on the tissue if the problem is leaf streak disease.

More detailed information can be found at http://www.aphis.usda.gov/npb/daylily.html and http://doacs.state.fl.us/~pi/enpp/pathology/daylily-rust.html and other sources. Call the extension office for specific recommendations if you suspect that your daylilies are infected with rust.

Rust Resistant Daylilies:

> Red Volunteer and Miss Mary Mary (All America Selections Winners), Over the Top, Burning Embers, Fairest of Them All, Escargot, Little Business, Mini Pearl, Butterscotch Ruffles, Mac the Knife, Yangtze, Holy Spirit, Black-Eyed Stella, Lullaby Baby, Bitsy, Frankly Scarlet, Plum Perfect

Photo by Daren Mueller, Iowa State University Extension

Hosta spp.
Hosta

Say: HOSS-tuh
Family: Liliaceae (Lily)
Other names: Funkia, plantain lily
Origin: Japan and China
Zones: 3–9
Light: Shade to partial shade

Water use zone: Moderate
Size: Varies from 6 inches to over 3 feet tall with a similar spread
Soil: Moist, organic, well-drained, neutral
Salt tolerance: Moderate

Hostas are grown primarily for their striking foliage. Leaves, which can be elliptic to heart-shaped, smooth or puckered, green, yellow, gray, or bluish with various kinds of variegations, grow into attractive mounds. In summer, flowers bloom on slender stalks held well above the foliage.

Right Place Growing hostas in the South requires careful attention to site and selection. Well-amended soil is a must, and the coolest, shadiest place in the landscape is the best place, provided competition with tree roots such as large oaks and magnolias is kept to a minimum. Performance is best in consistently moist soil, and mulch helps to maintain moisture and keeps the roots cool.

Continued Care Slugs, hail, wind, leaf spots, crown rot, and chewing insects can cause unsightly damage to hostas. Slugs, in particular, must be controlled. Gardeners in the Deep South might try growing some in pots where the roots have a better chance to obtain the chilling hours needed for best growth. Fertilize with slow release, high nitrogen fertilizer.

Propagation Division of established clumps every three to five years is the method of propagation most easily

accomplished by gardeners. It is possible to grow hosta from seed, and growers use tissue culture to grow thousands at a time.

Kinds There are as many as three thousand cultivars and 50 to 70 species of *Hosta*. Southern growers must select those that can withstand our heat and those that need the fewest hours of cold temperature. The following, though certainly not a complete list, were recommended by multiple sources: 'August Moon', 'Honeybells', 'Francee', 'Sum and Substance', 'Aphrodite', 'So Sweet', 'Sugar and Cream', 'Patriot', 'Blue Angel', 'Savannah', 'Fried Green Tomatoes', and 'Guacamole'.

Other Uses Use hostas in the shade of tall trees, in borders, and in woodland or natural gardens. The plants are good either massed or used as specimens. They are excellent in containers. Floral designers often make good use of the attractive foliage.

Liriope muscari
Border Grass

Say: Luh-RYE-oh-pee mus-KAR-ree
Family: Liliaceae (Lily)
Other names: Lilyturf, liriope, monkey grass
Origin: China, Taiwan, and Japan
Zones: 6–10

Light: Shade to partial shade
Water use zone: Moderate to low
Size: 10 to 30 inches and clumping
Soil: Moist, well-drained
Salt tolerance: Moderate

Dark green or variegated ribbon-like foliage that grows almost anywhere is liriope's claim to fame. Growing from 10 to 30 inches in length depending on the cultivar, it cascades toward the ground and forms rounded clumps. During the summer, white, lavender, or purple flowers that resemble hyacinths are held well above the foliage. Pea-sized black or white berries follow the flowers. Liriope makes a fine-textured, soft groundcover that will last for many years.

Right Place Liriope establishes best in well-worked, fertile soil. For fast coverage, plant in a gridlike pattern about ten inches apart. Mulch between clumps to maintain moisture and inhibit weed growth. When liriope is planted under deciduous trees, fallen leaves and debris often sift down through the foliage and are thus hidden. Although shade is preferred, liriope also grows in considerable sun and is tolerant of most soils.

Continued Care Mow in early spring before growth begins. Fertilize after mowing and apply mulch between clumps if needed. Water during periods of drought. Pre-emergent herbicides can be used to help prevent weed growth. Scale insects can be troublesome and may require treatment. As always read labels and follow directions carefully when applying any insecticide or herbicide.

Propagation Liriope can be divided at any time of year into clumps of any size to acquire additional plants. Berries germinate easily, but division is easier and quicker.

Kinds Many cultivars of *Liriope muscari* are in the trade. Choose 'Evergreen Giant' that grows to 18 inches tall, or 'Monroe White' if you want white flowers. 'Variegata' has yellow-striped leaves. 'Gold Banded', 'Majestic', 'Silvery Midget', 'Purple Bouquet', 'Christmas Tree', 'Big Blue', and others are available.

Other Uses Outline planting beds, paths, and walkways with this shape-defining plant. A dense root mass makes it an excellent choice for controlling erosion on sloping terrain. It is a good choice to fill in spaces in small parking lot islands or areas between the sidewalk and street.

Liriope spicata
Creeping Liriope

Say: luh-RYE-oh-pee spy-KAY-tuh
Family: Liliaceae (Lily)
Other names: Creeping lilyturf
Origin: China and Japan
Zones: 6–10

Light: Shade to partial shade
Water use zone: Moderate to low
Size: 6 to 12 inches and spreading
Soil: Moist, well-drained
Salt tolerance: Moderate

Choose *Liriope spicata* when an ornamental, evergreen, grasslike plant is needed to cover an area. Coverage will be quick as the plants spread by underground rhizomes to form colonies. Clusters of violet to white flowers that are somewhat hidden by the foliage bloom in mid to late summer. Blackish berries form in fall. Choose either the solid green form or a variegated form. A variegated cultivar is a good choice for lighting up a dark corner.

Right Place Best placement is a shady to partly shady spot under shrubs and trees. Avoid full sun, especially in areas with high summer temperatures. Although creeping liriope is drought tolerant once established, performance will be best in moist, fertile soil in a place out of the way of frequent foot traffic. Be aware that it may become invasive if not confined. A root barrier that is 18 inches deep is recommended to control spread.

Continued Care Mow in late winter before growth begins to remove unsightly foliage and to improve the appearance of the bed. Fertilize with a slow-release fertilizer when new growth begins in spring. Avoid watering late in the day to prevent diseases.

Propagation New plants are easy to obtain by dividing existing clumps or by removing offsets. New plants can be grown from seed if pulp is removed from the berrylike fruit before planting.

Kinds 'Silver Dragon' has slender, variegated green and white leaves and lavender flowers. 'Franklin Mint' has green foliage, pale lavender flowers, and leaves that are a little wider than the variegated cultivar. Both are able to out-compete other plants that attempt to grow in the same space. Swollen growths resembling small potatoes grow on the roots. This characteristic makes the species able to withstand considerable drought.

Other Uses *Liriope spicata* is used in mass plantings anywhere a spreading groundcover is needed. One particularly good use is along streams and ponds where it can help stabilize the soil.

Ophiopogon japonicus
Mondo Grass

Say: oh-fee-oh-POH-gon
    juh-PON-ih-kus
Family: Liliaceae (Lily)
Other names: Lilyturf, snakebeard
Origin: Japan, Korea
Zones: 7–11

Light: Shade to partial shade
Water use zone: Moderate to low
Size: Depends on variety—from 2 to
    12 inches tall and spreading
Soil: Fertile, well-drained
Salt tolerance: High

Mondo grass is an evergreen perennial that is grown for its foliage and groundcover effect. Nearly indestructible, it tolerates many garden situations, including standing water as well as drought. Some foot traffic is tolerated, and it is an excellent choice to plant underneath trees where tree roots interfere with mowing.

Plants grow in clumps, and leaves emerge from a web of rhizomes just below the soil surface. Although mondo grass can be confused with *Liriope*, its texture is finer. Unlike *Liriope*, which holds its flowers above the foliage, the flowers and berries of mondo grass remain hidden beneath the leaves.

Right Place Mondo grass grows in shade to part sun and prefers well-drained, moist soil. Space 6 to 12 inches apart for groundcover use. The species can become invasive in good soil, so solid boundaries are recommended to limit its spread. Cultivars are not as vigorous as the species.

Continued Care Usually fertilizer is not needed for adequate growth. Mow in late winter before new growth begins if needed to remove unsightly foliage. Edge if plants spread in unwanted places. Pests and diseases are not usually a concern.

Propagation More plants are easily obtained by dividing existing clumps.

Kinds Cultivars of *Ophiopogon japonicus* include 'Gyokuruu' (two inches tall, dark green), 'Nana' (four to five inches tall, compact, slow-growing), 'Shiroshima Ryu' (three to four inches tall with dark green and white striped leaves), and 'Variegatus' (six to ten inches tall, green and white striped leaves). Several species of *Ophiopogon* are popular as groundcovers. Some cultivars of *O. planiscapus* are nearly black. *O. jaburan* is the very popular Aztec grass that is used as a groundcover and foundation plant in many residential and commercial landscapes.

Other Uses Dwarf cultivars are excellent to use between stepping stones and to cover small, enclosed spaces. Tall selections are often used as foundation plantings, and small plants are sometimes used to underplant bonsai and other container plants.

Rubus pentalobus
Creeping Raspberry

Say: RUB-us pen-tah-LO-bus
Family: Rosaceae (Rose)
Other names: Crinkle-leaf creeper,
    creeping Taiwan bramble
Origin: Taiwan
Zones: 7–9

Light: Sun to partial shade
Water use zone: Low
Size: 3 to 6 inches tall by 3 to 6 feet
    in all directions
Soil: Well-drained
Salt tolerance: Unknown

Creeping raspberry is a fast-growing, evergreen groundcover. Dark green, finely puckered, leathery leaves grow about one and one-half inches wide and have three to five lobes. In fall and winter, the leaves turn dark bronze to burgundy. Insignificant white flowers bloom in summer, and tiny raspberry-like fruits are borne in late summer. Fruits are tasty and edible, but collecting enough for a pie might take a long time because they are very small. This groundcover was selected as a Georgia Gold Medal winner. It seems to thrive in harsh growing conditions and can tolerate fluctuations in soil moisture from very wet to very dry.

Right Place Choose a place in full sun to light shade with well-drained soil. Plant four to six feet apart to allow room for plants to spread. Apply granular fertilizer such as 16-4-8 or 12-4-8 in early spring, and water in thoroughly.

Continued Care Water regularly until plants are well established, and then water only during periods of drought. Mow in early spring to promote new growth if plants look ragged following a harsh winter. Avoid overhead irrigation and continuously wet soil. Remove weeds until plants grow together and are able to outgrow competing plants.

Propagation Separating rooted runners from existing plants offers an easy means of increase.

Kinds Creeping raspberry may still be listed by its former name, *Rubus calycinoides*. The cultivar 'Emerald Carpet' and 'Formosan Carpet' are the same according to the University of British Columbia. New growth is bright green. Another cultivar, 'Golden Quilt', puts out bright yellow new growth which turns green at maturity. Successive flushes give a bicolor effect all summer, turning to tricolor in fall when leaves begin to turn red.

Other Uses Plant this adaptable plant on tough sites, including hot, dry, erodible slopes. Take advantage of its growth habit by allowing it to cascade over the edge of a raised bed, planter, or container.

Saxifraga stolonifera
Strawberry Begonia

Say: saks-if-FRAG-uh sto-lo-NIF-er-uh
Family: Saxifragaceae (Saxifrage)
Other names: Strawberry geranium, roving sailor, creeping saxifrage
Origin: Japan, China
Zones: 7–10

Light: Shade to partial shade
Water use zone: Moderate
Size: 6 to 12 inches in bloom
Soil: Moist, organically rich
Salt tolerance: Slight

Despite its common names, strawberry begonia is neither a strawberry, nor a begonia, nor a geranium. Plants have two- to four-inch, roundish to heart-shaped leaves. Distinctive silvery veins decorate the tops of the leaves, and reddish, hairy undersides lend an extra dimension that is delightful to touch. Plants spread by sending out runners in the manner of strawberries. Lacy clusters of pink or white flowers bloom from spring to fall. Many people grow strawberry begonia as a houseplant and are surprised to learn that it is hardy in many areas of the country. Beautiful foliage and ability to spread rapidly make it a good groundcover.

Right Place Shade or part shade is preferred. Soil should be moisture retentive but well drained. Plant along paths under trees or other protective structures where its interesting texture and color can be best appreciated.

Continued Care Very little maintenance is needed. Flowers can be removed after they die, and some edging may be necessary to keep it in bounds. In the northern reaches of its hardiness range, strawberry begonia dies back to the roots in winter, but it is evergreen in most of Zones 8–10.

Propagation Strawberry begonia can be propagated by seed, division, or by rooting the trailing rosettes.

Kinds Several cultivars of *Saxifraga stolonifera* (syn. *S. sarmentosa*) are available. 'Tricolor' has striking foliage of hot pink, deep raspberry, white, and dark green. 'Kinki Purple' has rounded, purple-backed leaves that are covered in long red hair. Clumps send out foot-long, bright red threads that drop to the ground and sprout new plants where they land. 'Harvest Moon' has brilliant sulfur-yellow foliage with a red, metallic sheen. 'Athens' and 'Maroon Beauty' are also listed by some nurseries.

Other Uses Strawberry begonia has long been a favorite hanging basket plant. Runners hang over the edges in an attractive manner. Plants can be tucked in cracks in walls or between pavers or rocks.

Sedum acre
Goldmoss

Say: SEE-dum AK-ree
Family: Crassulaceae (Stonecrop)
Other names: Stonecrop, biting stonecrop, mossy stonecrop
Origin: Eurasia
Zones: 3–9

Light: Shade to partial shade
Water use zone: Low
Size: 4 to 6 inches and spreading
Soil: Well-drained
Salt tolerance: High

Bright yellow flowers in early spring are only one of *Sedum acre*'s attractions. More important is the evergreen foliage that retains its chartreuse color throughout the year. Goldmoss is very hardy, and it tolerates drought. As a matter of fact, it is very useful in poor, dry soils where little else will grow. A few reports of invasiveness, or at least exuberance, have been noted, but it has never been so in my garden.

Right Place Goldmoss prefers a place in full sun. Sandy or rocky soil is preferred, and well-drained soil is essential. Dampness over a long period will cause decline and rot.

Continued Care Seldom are any pests or diseases of any consequence to goldmoss. However, it cannot compete with weeds. Weeds must be hand-pulled, and oftentimes pieces of sedum are removed with the weeds. The plant is best in small, detailed areas where its fine texture can be appreciated.

Propagation Goldmoss roots from stem cuttings. Pieces of foliage that fall on the ground often root. To start a new groundcover, shred a few plants into a newly tilled area and cover lightly with soil. Water well. The newly planted sprigs should be

off to a good start in a few weeks.

Kinds *Sedum acre* var. *aurea,* or *S. acre* 'Aurea' is sometimes listed as a variety or cultivar of goldmoss sedum. Other trailing stonecrops include blue spruce stonecrop (*S. reflexum*) which has bluish-green, needlelike leaves; Kamschatca stonecrop (*S. kamtschaticum*) with yellow and/or red flowers and bronzed fall foliage; and our native wild or woods sedum (*S. ternatum*) with white, starlike flowers in branches of three, which is found in damp, woodsy sites.

Other Uses Goldmoss sedum is attractive planted in containers and walls where it cascades gracefully over the sides. It is a plant of choice for areas with little soil, such as rock gardens, or in small areas where unusual color or texture is needed.

Selaginella braunii syn. S. pellascens

Arborvitae Fern

Say: sell-lah-gi-NEL-uh BRAUN-e-eye
Family: Selaginellaceae (Spikemoss)
Other names: Club moss, spike
  moss, selaginella
Origin: Western China
Zone: 6–10

Light: Shade
Water use zone: Moderate
Size: 12 to 18 inches tall
Soil: Organic
Salt Tolerance: None

Even though people call this plant arborvitae fern, it is not a fern at all, but is a prehistoric fern relative called club moss. Since it is a vascular plant that produces spores, it is often mistaken for a fern.

Selaginella gradually grows to cover the ground with a solid mass that inhibits weed growth. Scaly foliage resembles that of arborvitae or cedar. Yellow green fronds of finely dissected foliage look delicate, but in fact the plant is a sturdy, well-suited workhorse in its shady nook.

Right Place Plant quart- or gallon-sized containers a foot or so apart in shade or filtered sunlight. Amend sand or heavy clay soil by incorporating a two- or three-inch layer of compost or humus. Although it likes moist, shady spots, it does not like standing water.

Continued Care Water as needed to maintain damp soil. If appearance is ragged following a severe winter, trim old or damaged fronds. New growth will quickly emerge. Fertilize in early spring just as new growth begins with all-purpose, slow-release fertilizer.

Propagation The club mosses can be divided easily at any time of year. Simply divide mature clumps and replant the divisions. Cuttings root easily if inserted in soil and kept damp. Club mosses can be grown from spores, but it is a complicated process that is usually done only in research laboratories.

Kinds About 700 to 800 species are found worldwide. Peacock fern (*Selaginella uncinata*) is a diminutive three- to six-inch tall club moss noted for its bluish-green iridescent leaves. Irish moss (*S. kraussiana* 'Aurea' grows about two inches tall and retains its bright golden color year-round. Gemmiferous spikemoss (*S. moellendorffii*) is an easy-to-grow Chinese species that bears tiny plantlets that drop off and form new colonies where they land.

Other Uses Selaginella looks great in hanging baskets or in containers skirting taller plants. Small varieties are useful in terrariums.

Trachelospermum asiaticum
Asiatic Jasmine

Say: tray-key-low-SPER-mum
ay-see-AT-ee-kum
Family: Apocynaceae (Dogbane)
Other names: Little-leaf jasmine,
dwarf jasmine
Origin: Southeast Asia
Zone: 7B–10

Light: Sun or shade
Water use zone: Low
Size: To 12 inches and spreading
Soil: Tolerant of most
Salt tolerance: Moderate

Frequently used as a groundcover in the South, Asiatic jasmine is best in areas where people do not walk. It has evergreen, leathery foliage on tough, vining stems. Foliage may have a reddish cast in winter. The smooth, reddish brown stems exude a milky liquid when broken.

Right Place Asiatic jasmine is tolerant of a wide variety of soils, and it does well in sun or shade. Plant 4-inch pots on 12-inch centers or gallon plants about 18 inches apart. Fertilize lightly and water regularly until established.

Continued Care After Asiatic jasmine is well established, it is very drought tolerant and has very low nutrient requirements. Keep in bounds by edging. Mow with the lawn mower on its highest setting once a year in early spring to limit the height of the jasmine and to promote a uniform appearance. Mowing will also permit more air movement and minimize the risk of disease caused by consistently wet foliage. Remove weeds regularly until established. Once established, weeds are not usually a problem. However, if necessary, Roundup can be used to control weeds after the jasmine is well-established and the foliage is mature.

Propagation Pieces of Asiatic jasmine can be rooted in water if one is patient. It can also be transplanted to other areas by cutting squares out of established beds that are growing thickly. Simply cut out a square along with the soil and move it to where it is wanted.

Kinds *Trachelospermum asiaticum* 'Tricolor' has variegated white, green, and red foliage. 'Variegatum' has cream or white variegation, and the J. C. Raulston Arboretum in North Carolina introduced a cultivar named 'Theta' which has very narrow leaves. *Trachelospermum jasminoides* (Confederate jasmine), a relative with very fragrant flowers, is better suited as a climbing vine.

Other Uses Use as a deer-resistant, drought-tolerant groundcover, a slope stabilizer, and lawn alternative. Allow it to cascade attractively down walls or sides of containers.

46

Tradescantia pallida 'Purpurea' syn. *Setcreasea pallida*

Purple Heart

Say: trad-es-KAN-tee-uh PAL-lid-duh
Family: Commelinaceae (Spiderwort or dayflower)
Other names: Purple queen, setcreasea
Origin: Mexico

Zone: 8–11 (7 if protected)
Light: Sun to partial shade
Water use zone: Low
Size: 12 inches tall and spreading
Soil: Well drained
Salt tolerance: High

Purple heart is a sprawling groundcover plant that has very purple, lance-shaped leaves and arching stems. Pale orchid-pink, three-petaled flowers emerge at stem tips during the summer. They are open only in the morning and are visually insignificant. Bright purple leaves give this plant its distinction. Stems are very brittle and easily broken.

Even though the dark purple of setcreasea is very noticeable in the landscape, it is a good mixer. Almost any color combines well with the purple plants in the garden.

Right Place Best leaf color and compactness is achieved in full sun, but some shade is tolerated. Give purple heart a place in well-drained soil. Root rot occurs if the soil is too wet. Use in a mass by itself to make a brightly colored groundcover over a long season.

Continued Care Once established, purple heart is drought tolerant. Extra irrigation is needed only during extremely dry spells. Cut back or remove dead foliage in early spring before new growth begins. Fertilize lightly at the beginning of the growing season with slow-release fertilizer. Trim as needed to keep in bounds.

Propagation Simply break off the stems and place them in damp soil or water. Roots will appear in a couple of weeks. Established clumps are easily divided and transplanted.

Kinds A variegated form is listed by Yucca Do Nursery in Texas. Leaves appear to be a lighter purple, and dark green streaks run down the length of the leaves.

Other Uses Purple heart is great as a color accent in mixed borders. Frequently it is used in hanging baskets and containers where it cascades over the sides. Few groundcovers are better suited for difficult dry areas such as under eaves and awnings. Reportedly purple heart is able to absorb toxic substances from soil, so it has potential as an accumulator plant for evaluating environmental pollution.

Tricyrtis hirta
Toad Lily

Say: try-SER-tis HER-tuh
Family: Liliaceae (Lily)
Other names: Tricyrtis
Origin: Asia
Zones: 5–9
Light: Shade

Water use zone: Moderate
Size: 24 to 30 inches by 18 to 24 inches
Soil: Moist, well-drained, humus rich
Salt tolerance: Unknown

Toad lily is a hardy perennial that blooms in fall. Orchidlike white blossoms flecked with purple are clustered in the leaf axils down the length of the stems. While the flowers are unusual and interesting, they are present for a short time. The arching form and row upon row of attractive, lance-shaped leaves are the main attractions. Roots are rhizomatous, and plants spread slowly to form modest clumps. Although slugs can occasionally be troublesome, plants are rabbit and deer resistant.

Right Place Plant toad lilies in moist, well-drained, slightly acid soil rich in organic matter. Best performance will be evidenced by plants grown in deep shade. For groundcover effect, place plants about three feet apart so that the arching form of each plant can be appreciated. Mulch well with organic mulch.

Continued Care Water as needed to maintain moisture. Fertilize in spring with balanced, slow-release fertilizer or organic foods like fish emulsion diluted to half strength. Overfertilization may cause burned leaf tips.

Propagation Toad lily can be divided in early spring before new growth begins. Lift the clump, separate the roots, and replant each division in humusy soil. Seeds can be planted but need stratification over the winter. In ideal situations, plants self seed. Stem cuttings taken in early summer root easily at stem nodes.

Root cuttings also yield new plants.

Kinds According to which taxonomist is consulted, the genus *Tricyrtis* has about 20 different species. *T. hirta* and *T. formosana* are commonly available, and *T. bakerii* and *T. flava* can sometimes be found at specialist nurseries. Among the other species are *T. macropoda, T. affinis, T. latifolia* and *T. macranthopsis.* Several named cultivars are offered by nurseries and mail-order sources. Wayside Gardens offers *T.* 'Miyazaki' and *T.* 'Amethystina'. There is also a variegated form which has leaves with cream-colored edges.

Other Uses Tricyrtis is excellent in shady borders, woodland gardens, and naturalized areas. Place along pathways where flowers can be seen at close range.

Chapter 2

Ferns as Groundcovers

Some of my favorite ferns are discussed in this section. Information about other ferns can be found on pages 116–122.

Athyrium filix-femina
Lady Fern

Say: uh-THEE-ree-um FY-liks
fem-in-uh
Family: Dryopteridaceae (Wood fern)
Other names: None
Origin: North America, Asia, Europe
Zones: 5–9
Light: Shade to partial shade

Water use zone: Moderate
Size: 1 to 3 feet tall by 1 to 3 feet wide
Soil: Organic, moist but well-drained
Salt Tolerance: None

Lady fern is a feathery light green fern with lacy twice-cut fronds that grow up to three feet long. It is distinguishable from other ferns by the pale J-shaped sori on the undersides of the leaf segments. Some say that the common name comes from the fact that these sori suggest the arched eyebrows of a pretty lady. Others believe that it is called lady fern because of its extreme variability which is reminiscent of some ladies' inclinations to change their minds.

Right Place Performance is best in shade to part shade. Some sun is tolerated if soil is kept moist. Soil should be fertile, slightly acid to neutral, and well drained. Lady fern is not as strong as other ferns, so place it in a protected place where children, dogs, and strong winds will not break the delicate fronds. Space 18 to 24 inches apart.

Continued Care Cut down dead fronds in late winter or early spring before new growth emerges. Fertilization is not necessary if soil is amended prior to planting and an organic mulch is maintained. Divide clumps in early spring every few years to reposition crowns at the soil level.

Propagation Division of rhizomes is the most common means of propaga-

tion. As with other ferns, it can also be started by spores, though this method is not commonly practiced by the average gardener.

Kinds Over 180 species and hundreds of cultivars of lady fern are available. European lady fern has many popular cultivars. Many species from Japan and other parts of Asia are available. Southern lady fern (*A. asplenioides*) is native to the southeastern United States and is a threatened species in Florida.

Other Uses Lady fern is at home along stream banks and on wooded slopes. It also occurs in meadows, open thickets, and swamps, and can colonize cracks in rocks and rock crevices. Few plants are as well-suited for naturalizing and massing in woodlands.

Cyrtomium falcatum

Holly Fern

Say: sir-TOH-mee-um fal-KAY-tum
Family: Dryopteridaceae (Wood fern)
Other names: Japanese or Asian
　holly fern
Origin: Asia, India, Southern Africa
　and Hawaii
Zones: 7–11

Light: Shade
Water use zone: Moderate
Size: 2 to 3 feet tall
Soil: Organic, acid
Salt Tolerance: Moderate

Lustrous, stiff, erect to arching fronds radiate out from the center of plants to form attractive clumps. Individual fronds grow from 20 to 30 inches long and up to eight inches wide. Although holly fern has been a very popular porch plant since the 1800s, it is equally suited to shady beds in the landscape.

Right Place Plant in partial to full shade underneath trees or structures and follow a regular watering schedule at least during the first growing season to establish a deep root system. Enrich poor soil with organic matter and mulch well to maintain moisture.

Continued Care Water regularly until plants are well established, after which time they are drought tolerant. Groom by removing dead fronds, but avoid cutting into or damaging the crown. Fertilize in early spring just as new growth begins with all-purpose, slow-release fertilizer. If container-grown, fertilize every six months with fish emulsion or water soluble fertilizer diluted to half strength.

Propagation Starting new plants from spores is not especially complicated. Simply deposit spores on the surface of sandy peat. Cover with glass or plastic and maintain moisture until new plants form. When plants are large enough to handle, they can be transplanted into individual containers. Established clumps usually do not need to be divided.

Kinds Several cultivars are available including dwarf versions and those with various shaped leaves. 'Butterfieldii' has deeply serrated leaf margins, 'Compactum' has leaves shorter than the species, and 'Rochfordianum' sports hollylike leaves with coarsely fringed margins.

Other Uses Holly fern can be used as a houseplant in bright light. Use it in shady gardens with hostas, impatiens, and caladiums, or with other ferns for a contrast in color and texture. Plant around large trees or shrubs. Use in cut arrangements if spore cases are green. Ripe clusters of spore cases split and shatter brown spores—on table cloths or whatever else they happen to be near.

Dryopteris erythrosora
Autumn Fern

Say: dry-OP-ter-ris
air-rith-roh-SOR-ruh
Family: Dryopteridaceae (Wood fern)
Other names: Copper shield fern,
shaggy shield fern, Japanese red
shield fern, Japanese wood fern
Origin: Japan, China, Korea
Zones: 5–9

Light: Shade to partial shade
Water use zone: Moderate to low
Size: 18 to 24 inches tall, spreading
12 to 15 inches wide
Soil: Moist (until well established),
humus rich, well-drained
Salt Tolerance: Slight

Selected as both a Florida Plant of the Year and a Georgia Gold Medal Winner, this evergreen fern is attractive in Southern gardens. Coppery-red and green triangular fronds emerge in spring and contrast pleasantly with older dark green fronds. As summer progresses, the fronds turn solid green.

Right Place Autumn fern does best in highly organic soils, so poor soils should be amended by adding organic matter. Planted on 18-inch centers, it will eventually cover the entire space with its graceful, upright fronds. Particularly drought tolerant once established, it does well under the dry shade of large trees.

Continued Care Until autumn fern is well established, it should not be allowed to dry out. At planting time, (preferably in the fall) apply a balanced fertilizer at the rate of one pound per 100 square feet and water in well. Fertilize again in spring before new fronds emerge. Removal of dead fronds each spring will keep the planting looking neat. Autumn fern is rarely bothered by pests or diseases.

Propagation Autumn fern spreads slowly by short, creeping rhizomes. It is a clumping fern, so division of mature clumps is the easiest means of propagation for the home gardener.

Kinds A cultivar aptly named 'Brilliance' offers more brilliant color and is reported to hold its coloration even at maturity. A variety called *Dryopteris erythrosora* var. *purpurascens* (syn. *Dryopteris purpurella*) grows much larger, with fronds reaching three feet or more. Dark evergreen fronds emerge bright cinnamon red in spring and summer.

Other Uses Autumn Fern is most at home in shaded woodland gardens, but it can also be used as an accent plant. It makes an excellent backdrop for flowering shade plants, and can even be used in a shady foundation planting or in a container.

Polystichum polyblepharum

Tassel Fern

Say: pol-IS-tick-um
  pol-ee-BLEF-ar-um
Family: Dryopteridaceae (Wood fern)
Other names: Japanese tassel fern,
  bristle fern, Korean tassel fern,
  Japanese lace fern
Origin: Japan, Southern Korea
Zones: 5–9

Light: Shade to partial shade
Water use zone: Moderate
Size: 12 to 18 inches tall spreading
  to 24 inches
Soil: Evenly moist, humus-rich, well-
  drained, acid
Salt Tolerance: Slight

Tassel fern is a broad, symmetrical, vase-shaped, evergreen plant. Lustrous, dark green, double-cut fronds arch out from a central crown. Frosted undersides and rusty brown, hairy stems make it easy to identify. Fiddleheads begin unfurling like most other ferns, but as they unfurl they flip backward. At this stage the frond resembles a tassel, and it stays that way for several days. Other ferns open upward and outward, but they never dangle like the tassel fern. The name *polyblepharum* means "many eyelashes," which helps to explain the hairy-looking appendages on the stems.

Right Place A site in full to dappled shade suits tassel fern. It appreciates evenly moist, humus-rich, well-drained acidic soil. Plant about two feet apart to allow it to reach its full size and display its beautiful arching form to best advantage.

Continued Care Fertilize tassel fern at planting time with a sprinkling of balanced fertilizer (about a pound per 100 square feet). Keep soil evenly moist. Although the fronds are long-lasting and usually last for more than a year, unsightly ones may need to be removed in the spring before new ones emerge to keep the planting well groomed. If needed, the entire plant can be cut down in spring before growth begins.

Propagation Tassel fern has a clumping crown that slowly grows larger by creeping rhizomes. Propagation is easily accomplished by dividing the clump in spring. Plant divisions in soil enriched by the addition of organic matter if soil is not already humus rich.

Kinds There are many species of *Polystichum*. Sometimes tassel fern is listed as *Polystichum setosum,* which is a synonym or former name.

Other Uses Tassel fern is most frequently used in shady borders and woodland gardens. However, it can be grown in a container if kept in bright light (no direct sun). Fronds are frequently used in cut flower arrangements.

Rumohra adiantiformis
Leatherleaf fern

Say: roo-MOH-ruh
    ad-ee-an-tih-FOR-mis
Family: Dryopteridaceae (Wood fern)
Other names: Leather fern, seven
    week fern, iron fern, Baker fern
Origin: South Africa, South America,
    New Zealand, Australia
Zones: 8–11

Light: Shade
Water use zone: Moderate
Size: 1 to 3 feet tall by 4 to 5 feet
    wide
Soil: Organic, Acid
Salt Tolerance: Moderate

Leatherleaf fern is the greenery most often included in a bouquet of roses or other flowers from the florist. Cut fronds last up to a month in water. In the ground, dense mats form as plants spread by underground stolons, so it makes an excellent groundcover in areas where it is hardy. Triangular, leathery, evergreen fronds grow at a moderate rate and densely enough to crowd out most competition.

Right Place Plant leatherleaf fern in a mostly shaded place in organic soil. Protect from extreme cold, for it is hardy only to about 25°F. For groundcover use, plant on 18- to 24-inch centers.

Continued Care Fertilize in spring and again in summer if needed to maintain a dark green color. Keep the foliage dry as much as possible to prevent fungal diseases. Although leatherleaf fern is relatively drought tolerant, it will benefit from a good watering during periods of drought. Pests do not usually affect the health of the plants.

Propagation Division of rhizomes is the best way for gardeners to get additional plants. Establishment may take a bit longer than other ferns, because it resents disturbance. New plants can also be started from spores sown on sterilized moist peat.

Kinds No cultivars of leatherleaf fern were listed in any references. *Aspidium capense* and *Rumohra aspidioides* are synonyms or former names. According to John T. Mickel in *Ferns for American Gardens*, this is the only species in the *Rumohra* genus.

Other Uses Leatherleaf fern is used in masses for naturalizing. Large scale commercial plantings in Florida and South America provide cut foliage for the florist industry. Even though leatherleaf fern grows well in containers, it is not among the most popular for hanging baskets because its form is upright instead of cascading or weeping.

Chapter 3
Shrubs as Groundcovers

People use shrubs extensively throughout their landscapes. Some have learned that many of the low-growing species make excellent groundcovers. As a rule, shrubs are not as aggressive as plants that spread by stolons or root where stems touch the ground. Many shrubs can serve as well-mannered, easy-care groundcover elements in the landscape.

Cephalotaxus harringtonia 'Prostrata'
Prostrate Japanese Plum Yew

Say: sef-uh-loh-TAKS-us
    har-ring-TOH-nee-uh
Family: Cephalotaxaceae (Plum yew)
Other names: Prostrate cow's tail
    pine
Origin: Japan, Korea, and China
Zones: 6–9
Light: Shade to partial shade

Water use zone: Moderate
Size: 2 to 4 feet tall by 6 to 10 feet
    wide
Soil: Well-drained, sandy, slightly
    acidic
Salt tolerance: Unknown

Prostrate Japanese plum yew is a spreading, wide-growing shrub. Each plant has many wide-reaching branches. Branches have many branchlets on which grow needle-like leaves that are flattened except for the V-shaped trough that they form. Fruit is a plumlike naked seed produced on female plants. This plant is a winner of both the Georgia Gold Medal and Pennsylvania Horticultural Society's Gold Medal Plant Award.

Right Place Plum yew is one of the best needled evergreens for use in the shade. It needs well-drained soil and is hardy as well as heat tolerant.

Continued Care Plum yews are slow to establish and require careful attention for about two years. Once established, however, they are relatively drought tolerant and carefree. Fertilize lightly in spring with slow-release fertilizer.

Propagation Although the dioecious plants sometimes bear infertile seeds in the absence of male plants, both male and female plants are needed if fruit and fertile seeds are desired. New plants can be started from seeds or cuttings, but patience is required because growth is slow. Division of self-layered stems and suckers is also a source of additional plants.

Kinds In addition to the prostrate cultivar of *Cephalotaxus,* upright forms are available that grow up to 30 feet tall and 20 feet wide. 'Duke Gardens' grows two to three feet tall and three to four feet wide.

'Fastigiata' is a columnar form with bottle-brush-like leaves that will grow about eight to ten feet tall and six to eight feet wide. A variety, *C. harringtonia* var. *dupacea* grows about 15 feet tall and has shorter needles than the species. The cultivar 'Korean Gold' has yellow- to gold-tipped foliage.

Other Uses Deer do not eat plum yews, so they are excellent additions to gardens where deer are problems. Even squirrels seem to dislike the fruit, which is edible raw as well as cooked.

Gardenia augusta 'Prostrata'

Trailing Gardenia

Say: gar-DEEN-ee-uh au-GUS-tah
Family: Rubiaceae (Madder)
Other names: Cape jasmine, dwarf gardenia, gardenia
Origin: China
Zones: 7B–10
Light: Partial shade

Water use zone: Moderate
Size: 2 to 3 feet tall by 4 to 6 feet wide
Soil: Moist, well-drained, organic
Salt tolerance: Slight

Few plants offer flowers as fragrant as those of a gardenia. Even though considerable maintenance is required to keep shrubs healthy, they are very popular in the South. Lustrous, dark green leaves borne on the horizontal branches of trailing gardenia make an excellent background for the creamy white flowers. Fruit is a small, relatively inconspicuous berry.

Right Place Gardenias will do well in partial shade. They require well-drained, acid soil high in organic matter. Maintain moisture, for they will abort flower buds if they become drought stressed. Protect from extreme winter temperatures as they can be damaged by cold in the northern part of their hardiness range. Plant near a patio or where the fragrance can be enjoyed.

Continued Care Keep gardenias well mulched. Fertilize with a complete, slow-release fertilizer in early spring and again in early fall at the rate of approximately half a pound per 100 square feet. If leaves turn yellow, it may indicate that the soil is not acid enough. This can be helped by adding elemental sulfur to the soil or by foliar applications of iron. Many insects and diseases plague gardenias. See page 58 for more information.

Propagation Gardenias can be successfully started by cuttings taken in June, July, and August. Take four- to five-inch tip cuttings and stick in a well-drained potting mix. Keep damp until new growth indicates that roots have formed.

Kinds Dwarf forms of *Gardenia augusta* (syn. *Gardenia jasminoides*) are commonly used as groundcovers. 'Radicans' (also known as 'Prostrata') is a small-leaved, almost creeping version of the species. *G. augusta* 'Radicans Variegata' is a variegated version with white leaf margins (pictured above).

Many cultivars of gardenia are in existence, and they vary in flower size and form, blooming time and duration, and shrub habit and size.

Other Uses Gardenias are effectively used as screens, hedges, borders, or specimen plants. Dwarf varieties are often used in bonsai.

Gardenia Pests and Diseases

Several insects attack gardenias. The ones that cause the most injury are scales, aphids, whiteflies, spider mites, and thrips. Sooty mold, a black, smut-like substance, grows on leaves if plants are infested with these insects. The mold does not injure the plant except by preventing sunlight from reaching the leaf, thereby interfering with photosynthesis. Mold grows on honey-dew secreted by the insects. Insecticidal soap and horticultural oil are often used to manage the pests. Contact your Cooperative Extension Service office for more controls.

Root-knot nematodes are also troublesome. In areas with mild winters (no colder than 28°F), gardenias are often grafted on *Gardenia thunbergia* rootstock, which resists root-knot nematode. For areas with colder winters, the most effective treatment for nematodes is to add copious amounts of organic matter to the soil. Natural enemies of the nematodes thrive in organic-rich soil, and gardenias grow more strongly and are thus more able to ward off insect attacks.

Stem canker is a serious gardenia disease which occurs at the soil line on the main stem. Since the disease organism enters the plant through wounds, every precaution should be taken to prevent damaging the stems. No controls are available, so infected plants should be destroyed.

For more in-depth information, download Circular 1098, "Gardenias" by Joan Bradshaw, or Fact Sheet FPS-223 by Edward F. Gilman. Both are publications of the Institute of Food and Agricultural Sciences at the University of Florida and can be found on the website at http://hort.ifas.ufl.edu.

Sooty mold
Photo courtesy of Theresa Friday

Ilex crenata 'Border Gem'
Japanese Holly

Say: EYE-lecks kre-NAY-tuh
Family: Aquifoliaceae (Holly)
Other names: none
Origin: Japan, Korea
Zones: 5–8
Light: Sun to partial shade

Water use zone: Moderate
Size: 1 foot tall with diligent pruning for groundcover use; spreads wider than tall
Soil: Well-drained, moisture retentive
Salt tolerance: Moderate to high

Japanese hollies are popular landscape plants because of their lustrous dark evergreen leaves and dense growth. At least 60 cultivars are available, most of which are not suitable for use as a groundcover, but which are, nevertheless, some of our most useful landscape plants. Flowers and berries are insignificant. The species grows up to 20 feet tall and wide after many years. The cultivar recommended as a groundcover is *Ilex crenata* 'Border Gem'.

Right Place Japanese hollies prefer sun but have some tolerance to shade. Soil acidity from 4.5–6.0 is tolerated, and well-drained, moisture retentive, highly organic, fertile soil is preferred. Fertilize at planting time by sprinkling 2 or 3 pounds of all purpose, slow release fertilizer per 100 square feet of bed.

Continued Care If soil was amended at planting time, additional fertilizer is usually not needed. Prune or clip any time of the year except in late summer or early fall. Mulch with an organic material like pine needles or bark chips.

Scale insects, spider mites, and nematodes may prove troublesome. Ask for treatment options at your Cooperative Extension Service office.

Propagation Japanese holly can be started from cuttings. However, cuttings grow very slowly and require special treatment. Consequently, it is best to purchase nursery-grown stock.

Kinds Japanese hollies come in all sizes and shapes. Some popular selections include: 'Helleri' (two feet tall and three to six feet wide); 'Compactum', (Round shaped to five feet); 'Skypencil' (ten to twelve feet tall and two to three feet wide; 'Soft Touch' (two feet by two feet); 'Stokes' (two and a half feet tall by five feet wide). Choose a cultivar to suit the purposes for which it is intended.

Other Uses Japanese hollies lend themselves to many uses in the landscape. They make excellent hedges, topiary designs, foundation plantings, and specimen plants. Some of the small-growing cultivars are excellent container plants.

Juniperus chinensis var. *sargentii*

Sargent's Juniper

Say: jew-NIP-er-us chi-NEN-sis var. sar-JEN-tee-eye
Family: Cupressaceae (Cypress)
Other names: Chinese juniper
Origin: Japan, China, Mongolia
Zones: 4–10
Light: Sun

Water use zone: Moderate
Size: 12 to 24 inches tall and spreading 7 to 9 feet wide
Soil: Alkaline to acidic, moist, well-drained
Salt tolerance: High

Sargent's juniper is one of the best Chinese junipers for ground-cover use because it is resistant to juniper blight that afflicts many junipers. Low-growing and wide-spreading, plants cover an area solidly with whiplike branches. Foliage is thick and varies in color from bright green to bluish-green depending on the cultivar.

Right Place Sargent's juniper is found on seashores and rocky, mountainous cliffs in its native region. It is tolerant of both acidic and alkaline soils, and full sun is preferred. Although drought tolerant once established, preference is for moist, well-drained soils. New plantings should be watered regularly for the first year. Be sure to space plants six to nine feet apart to allow space for plants at maturity. If planted too closely, a thick layer of foliage can form which leads to poor air circulation and increased vulnerability to pests and diseases.

Continued Care Avoid heavy pruning, as old wood will not produce new growth. Tip prune and thin as needed, but do not cut back to large limbs. Pruning out old, dead foliage underneath often contributes to better air circulation and thus better health. Fertilize with a complete fertilizer such as 16-4-8 at the rate of half a pound per 100 square feet in early spring. Irrigate thoroughly after fertilizing.

Propagation Cuttings root readily, and long limbs can be layered where they touch the soil.

Kinds Many species of Chinese juniper are used in gardens worldwide. Sizes range from tiny, ground-hugging plants to tree-sized specimens. Many authorities consider *Juniperus sargentii* to be a different species from *J. chinensis.* Since Michael Dirr states that he is no position to argue, I will not argue, either. Even so, several distinct cultivars of Sargent's juniper are available, including 'Compacta', 'Glauca' (bluish green foliage), and 'Veridis' (light green foliage).

Other Uses Sargent's juniper is excellent on slopes or draping over raised planters or containers.

Juniperus conferta
Shore Juniper

Say: jew-NIP-er-us kon-FER-tuh
Family: Cupressaceae (Cypress)
Other names: Japanese shore juniper
Origin: Japan
Zones: 5–10
Light: Sun

Water use zone: Moderate to low
Size: 12 to 18 inches tall by 10 feet wide
Soil: Alkaline to acidic, dry, sandy
Salt tolerance: High

Shore juniper is a dense, fine-textured, evergreen shrub with soft but sharp-tipped, awl-shaped needles. Fruit is a dark blue to silvery three-seeded cone one-third to half an inch in diameter. Reddish brown bark is often hidden by thick, overlapping needles. The landscape effect is that of a soft, feathery sea of green. Because of its salt tolerance, it makes an excellent groundcover near the sea.

Right Place Plant gallon-sized containers five or six feet apart for groundcover effect. Choose a place with full sun and sandy, well-drained soil.

Continued Care Shore juniper is usually a low-maintenance plant. Be sure that it has adequate room to grow. Water in early morning so that foliage will not remain wet any longer than necessary. Although some fertilizer is needed, over-fertilization may cause abundant soft growth that is susceptible to fungal diseases. Prune out diseased branch tips and destroy, but avoid excessive pruning.

Propagation Branches can be layered where they touch the soil, or tip cuttings can be taken.

Kinds 'Blue Pacific' (one foot high by six to eight feet wide) has blue-green foliage, a dense, compact habit, and great heat tolerance.

'Emerald Sea' (two feet tall by ten feet wide) has soft, green foliage, a looser habit, and greater cold tolerance than other cultivars. 'Silver Mist' (one to one and a half feet high by three to four feet wide) sports silvery blue-green foliage that takes on a bronze to purplish cast in winter. If bright yellow splashes of needles interspersed among blue-green foliage sounds attractive, choose 'Sunsplash' (also known as 'Variegata' and 'Akebono'). 'Irozam' is alleged to be tolerant of harsh, dry conditions and exposure to salt. Expect it to grow about one foot tall and six feet wide.

Other Uses Allow shore juniper to drape over walls or planters. Use it for seaside plantings, on roadsides, or on slopes to control erosion. Floral designers value the fragrant evergreen branches in seasonal crafts and designs.

Lantana

Say: lan-TAN-a kuh-MAR-uh
Family: Verbenaceae (Verbena)
Other names: Shrub verbena
Origin: West Indies
Zones: 8–11
Light: Sun
Water use zone: Moderate to low

Size: Varies with cultivar from 1 to 6 feet tall and wide
Soil: Slightly acid with moderate fertility; tolerates poor soil
Salt tolerance: High

Low, spreading cultivars of *Lantana camara* are among the most commonly grown groundcovers. Plants are covered with two-inch, disk-shaped flower heads throughout the summer. These flowers are attractive to butterflies. Choose a sterile cultivar so that viable seeds will not be produced and invasiveness will not be a problem. Be aware that the plants are extremely poisonous and deaths have been reported throughout its range.

Right Place Although lantana prefers a place in full sun and well-drained, moderately fertile soil, it is tolerant of poor soil and drought. Plants should be watered well until they are established and roots have spread into surrounding soil. Lantana is commonly chosen for areas near the beach and other bodies of salt water for its tolerance of salt.

Continued Care Although lantana is drought tolerant, it benefits from being watered during periods of dry weather. Avoid overhead watering which can encourage diseases and root rot. Prune during the summer by lightly shearing the tip growth to encourage repeat blooming. If plants become too large for their space, they can be pruned back by up to a third of their height and spread. Nutritional needs are low, but a light fertilization in spring will be beneficial. Whiteflies, mites, caterpillars, and lantana lace bugs may need to be controlled.

Propagation Sterile cultivars are propagated by cuttings. If seeds are viable, the plant should be destroyed.

Kinds Common lantana is a serious weed in 25 countries. It is a worldwide invader that has altered habitats and threatens to eliminate populations of native plants and animals. In Florida it has contaminated the gene pool of the three species of native lantana. Homeowners are strongly encouraged to remove and destroy existing plants. For landscape use, choose sterile cultivars such as 'Gold Mound', 'New Gold', 'Alba', and 'Patriot'.

Other Uses Use spreading cultivars to trail over walls and containers.

Lantana montevidensis

Trailing Lantana

Say: lan-TAN-a mon-tay-vid-EN-sis
Family: Verbenaceae (Verbena)
Other names: Weeping lantana
Origin: South America
Zones: 8B–11
Light: Sun
Water use zone: Moderate

Size: 6 to 12 inches tall; spreading to 6 feet
Soil: Prefers moderate fertility but tolerates poor soil
Salt tolerance: High

Weeping, vinelike stems make an attractive groundcover. Foliage may turn red to purple in colder months. Leaves are very malodorous and irritate the skin of some people. Tops die back at about 20° F, but plants will recover in the spring. Flowering is nonstop from spring through fall, or year-round in frost-free areas. Flowers are borne in clusters about one and a half inches wide.

Right Place Trailing lantana prefers full sun. Although it is tolerant of poor soils and drought, better performance can be expected if it is watered weekly. Be sure that the soil is well-drained. It has outstanding heat, wind, and salt tolerance, and deer do not prefer it. Nectar-laden blossoms make it a natural choice for butterfly gardens.

Continued Care Maintenance is minimal but pruning can be done to keep *Lantana montevidensis* within bounds. It is okay to stub it back to the ground occasionally, especially in spring to remove dead branches. It is resistant to lantana lacebug which mars the beauty of some of the other lantana species. It may, however, be attacked by whiteflies and spider mites. Lantana is not a heavy feeder.

One light application of fertilizer in spring is usually sufficient.

Propagation Cuttings can be taken from firm young shoots in spring, or hardwood cuttings can be taken in fall just before frost or cold weather kills it to the ground. New plants are easy to start by layering. Seeds can also be planted.

Kinds The species of weeping lantana is available with white, pink, and lavender flowers. Cultivars exist, such as 'Malan's Gold' which sports yellow and green foliage and rose-colored flowers. 'Pot of Gold' has bright yellow flowers. 'White Lightning' has pure white flowers, and 'Lavender Swirl' has white flowers that gradually deepen to pale lavender and finally rich lavender.

Other Uses Trailing lantana is excellent for use in large planters or hanging baskets where it is allowed to trail over the edge.

Nandina domestica 'Firepower'
Dwarf Nandina

Say: nan-DEE-nuh doh-MES-tic-uh
Family: Berberidaceae (Barberry)
Other names: Heavenly bamboo
Origin: Japan, China, India
Zones: 6–9
Light: Sun to partial shade

Water use zone: Moderate
Size: 2 feet tall and wide
Soil: Acid to slightly alkaline
Salt tolerance: Slight to none

'Firepower' is an evergreen shrub with attractive, compound leaves. The Florida Nurserymen and Growers Association once named it a "Plant of the Year."

Dwarf nandina 'Firepower' and other cultivars give the South some of its most dependable year-round color. In spring, the plants flush lime green. During the summer, foliage becomes tinged with red, and by fall it is bright red.

Right Place Dwarf nandinas appreciate well-drained soil that is slightly acidic to slightly alkaline. Although best color will be attained in full sun, they also grow well in partial shade. Plant two to three feet apart for a solid mass of color in the landscape. Once established, the plants are drought tolerant and heat resistant.

Continued Care Nandinas have no serious pests and require little maintenance. Mulch to keep the ground cool and moist. Apply a slow release fertilizer in spring if needed. Water during prolonged periods of drought.

Propagation The dwarf cultivars are usually started at the commercial level by tissue culture.

Kinds The non-fruiting dwarf nandinas, unlike their berry-producing parents and kin, do not pose a danger to natural habitats. *Nandina domestica* is listed as a Category I

exotic invasive plant for north Florida by the Florida Exotic Pest Plant Council. Berries, which are carried into natural areas by birds, sprout and proliferate.

Many other dwarf cultivars are available. 'Gulf Stream' or 'Compacta Nana' (three to four feet tall) has dark blue-green summer foliage that turns red in winter. 'Nana' (aka 'Nana Purpurea' and 'Atropurpurea Nana') grows to two feet and has leaves that are cupped or rolled (caused by a virus). 'Woods Dwarf' is similar, but without the virus effects of 'Nana'. 'Filamentosa' (also known as 'San Gabriel') has very lacy, deeply cut leaves.

Other Uses Dwarf nandina is useful anywhere a small, evergreen, colorful shrub could be placed, such as in beds, containers, or planters. Floral designers often use the foliage for arrangements "in the Oriental manner."

Pittosporum tobira 'Wheeleri'
Dwarf Pittosporum

Say: pit-uss-POR-um toe-BYE-ruh
Family: Pittosporaceae (Pittosporum)
Other names: Wheeler's pittosporum, Japanese mock orange
Origin: Japan
Zones: 8B–11
Light: Sun to partial shade

Water use zone: Moderate
Size: 2 to 3 feet tall by 3 to 5 feet wide
Soil: Organic, moist but well-drained
Salt tolerance: High

Wheeler's dwarf pittosporum is an evergreen shrub which forms a compact mound of dark green foliage. Insignificant but pleasantly scented flowers bloom in spring. Use this plant at the foreground of shrub borders, or plant it behind annuals to provide a dark green background against which the colorful flowers will show to best advantage. Avoid planting Wheeler's dwarf in areas where it will be brushed against. Branches are very brittle and break easily.

Right Place Plant on four-foot centers for groundcover use. Be sure that the site has excellent drainage and that the planting area has been amended with organic matter. Full sun, a place with good air circulation, and drip irrigation combine to inhibit leaf spot diseases that sometimes plague dwarf pittosporum.

Continued Care Careful placement as noted above is of prime importance to the welfare of this plant. Continued upkeep includes careful attention to nutritional and moisture needs. Use of slow-release fertilizer will provide adequate nutrition. Although soil must be well-drained, plants must not be allowed to become too dry. Use an organic mulch to help keep the soil evenly moist and to improve soil structure. Protect from severe temperatures.

Plants can be severely injured or outright killed at 10°F. No pruning is needed to keep plants neat and uniform.

Propagation Dwarf pittosporum can be propagated by semi-hardwood or hardwood cuttings.

Kinds The large species, *Pittosporum tobira,* usually grows 10–12 feet tall, but specimens up to 25 feet tall have been reported. The species can be grown as a large, spreading shrub, or it can be limbed up and grown as a tree. The cultivar 'Variegata' has gray-green leaves edged with white. Fragrant white flowers are borne in spring.

Other Uses Dwarf pittosporum is excellent in containers where it can be pruned into a small, picturesque, miniature tree, or it can be grown in its usual mounding form.

Raphiolepis spp.

Indian Hawthorn

Say: raff-fee-oh-LEPP-iss
Family: Rosaceae (Rose)
Other names: Yeddo hawthorn
Origin: India, Southern China
Zones: 7B–9B

Light: Sun
Water use zone: Moderate to low
Size: Varies with cultivar
Soil: Well-drained
Salt tolerance: High

Indian hawthorns used as groundcovers are small evergreen shrubs that are grown primarily for their neat, rounded form and attractive clusters of white or pink spring flowers. Small purplish-black berries appear after bloom and often persist all winter. Leathery, evergreen, two- to three-inch long, rounded leaves that cluster at the ends of branches turn purplish in winter.

Right Place Soil must be well-drained, and performance is best if plants receive at least six hours of sun each day. Provide good air circulation around plants, and be sure to choose cultivars that have resistance to Entomosporium leafspot. Excellent salt and drought tolerance makes Indian hawthorn a good choice for coastal gardens.

Continued Care Prune after flowering, if desired, for compact growth. Fertilize in spring with all-purpose fertilizer at the rate of one pound per 100 square feet of bed. Avoid overhead irrigation, and be sure that foliage stays dry as much as possible. Scale, fireblight, and leafspot diseases may be problematic.

Propagation Indian hawthorn can be started from cuttings taken about midsummer or from seeds.

Kinds Several cultivars range in mature size from two feet tall to the 12-foot-tall 'Majestic Beauty' and 'Rosalinda'. Confusion exists over whether many cultivars are of

Raphlolepis indica or *R. umbellata*. In reality, many familiar cultivars seem to be a hybrid of both species (*Raphiolepis* x *delacourii*). To add confusion, the species name is sometimes spelled "Raphiolepsis."

Of greater importance than the scientific name is the disease resistance. Various universities throughout the South have identified several cultivars that are resistant to Entomosporium leafspot. Among the most resistant cultivars are: 'Yedda', 'Indian Princess', 'Olivia', and 'Eskimo'. Showing good resistance are 'Blueberry Muffin', 'Clara', 'Georgia Charm', 'Georgia Petite', 'Betsy', 'Jack Evans', 'Majestic Beauty', and 'Snow White'.

Other Uses Use small cultivars in low dividers, containers, mass plantings, or foundation plantings. Large cultivars can be trained as standards and grown as small trees. These larger cultivars make excellent hedges, mass plantings, or screening.

Rhododendron eriocarpum
Satsuki Azalea

Say: roh-do-DEN-dron
   er-ee-oh-KAR-pum
Family: Ericaceae (Heath)
Other names: Gumpo azalea
Origin: Japan
Zones: 7–9

Light: Partial shade
Water use zone: Moderate
Size: Varies with cultivar; usually 2
   feet tall by 3 feet wide
Soil: Organic, acid
Salt tolerance: Moderate

The compact, evergreen Satsuki azaleas bloom later than most other azaleas. Dense foliage and slow growth make them desirable landscape plants, especially grown en masse. Many different flower colors are available. Some have flecks and specks, and some are striped, two-toned, or patterned. Flower size ranges from one and a half to three inches wide, but flowers are often partly hidden by the foliage. Foliage is generally smaller than other azalea species. Satsuki means 'fifth month' and refers to the fifth month of the lunar calendar. Expect flowers in May and June.

Right Place Azaleas prefer well-drained, acid soil (pH 4.5–5.5) that is rich in organic matter. Give them a place in partial, shifting shade, and be sure that they are protected from strong winter sun and wind.

Plant azaleas at or above the depth they grew in the nursery container, and do not let them dry out, particularly during the first year.

Continued Care Follow a regular watering schedule. Keep roots cool with a two- to three-inch layer of mulch. Feed with an acid forming fertilizer with micro nutrients after bloom and again during the summer and early fall at the rate of three quarters of a pound to one and a half pounds per 100 square feet. Control lacebugs, leafminers, spider mites, scale, and other common azalea pests and diseases. Prune after flowering if needed to control height.

Propagation Start new plants by taking three- to four-inch cuttings after spring growth has hardened. Layering easy to accomplish and often occurs naturally where the low-growing stems touch the ground.

Kinds Hundreds of cultivars of Satsuki azaleas are in existence. They were first introduced into the United States in the early 1900s. Michael Dirr lists Satsuki hybrids and Gumpos separately. However, he states that the gumpos are selections of *R. eriocarpum.* Very popular are the pink, white, and red gumpos.

Other Uses Low-growing Satsuki azaleas are ideal front-of-the-border plants. They are also excellent container plants and popular bonsai subjects.

Chapter 4

Native Groundcovers

By choosing native plants as groundcovers, we often make our gardens easier to maintain. After all, the native plants have fended for themselves for eons. They have lived and coexisted with the diseases, insects, and extremes of the Southern climate. Still, it is important to select plants to suit the site on which they are to grow. Luckily, many of the groundcovers native to the South are quite beautiful and make attractive additions to the garden.

Conradina canescens

Wild Rosemary

Say: kon-ruh-DEE-nuh kan-ESS-enz

Family: Lamiaceae (Mint)

Other names: Beach rosemary, minty rosemary, false rosemary, scrub mint

Origin: West Florida and coastal Alabama and Mississippi

Zones: 7–9

Light: Sun to partial shade

Water use zone: Low

Size: 1 to 3 feet tall and wide

Soil: Dry, well-drained

Salt tolerance: High

False rosemary is a shrubby ever-green perennial that is endemic to dunes and scrub areas of west Florida and coastal Alabama and Mississippi. Narrow, needlelike aromatic leaves are less than one inch long and are olive green with grayish undersides. Plants are reminiscent of very fine and lax or soft rosemary. In spring, clusters of white to lavender two-lipped flowers resembling small, pale lavender snapdragons bloom in profusion.

Right Place False rosemary is at home in poor, sandy, perfectly drained soil in a sunny to mostly sunny location. It is frequently used in beach restoration projects following hurricanes. Find the hottest, driest place possible and space plants three to five feet apart.

Continued Care Provide supplemental irrigation until established. Afterwards no care is needed for this native plant. Remove competing plants that might shade out or otherwise compete with the wild rosemary.

Propagation Plant fresh seeds or collect softwood cuttings during the growing season. Stick cuttings in a damp, well-drained propagation mix, and do not allow them to dry out. Move up to larger containers as necessary to develop a full rootball. Prune while small to promote branching. Plant in the landscape when the canopy has grown about six to eight inches tall.

Kinds There is only one *Conradina*

canescens, but other allopatric species (ones that do not interbreed because they are geographically isolated from one another) have been identified. Several of them are listed as federally endangered or threatened. Falling into that category are *C. etonia* (Etonia rosemary), *C. glabra* (Apalachicola rosemary), *C. verticillata* (Cumberland rosemary), *C. grandiflora* (large-flowered rosemary) and *C. brevifolia* (short-leafed rosemary).

Value to Wildlife Wild rosemary contributes to the habitat of the beach mouse. Flowers provide nectar for butterflies, hummingbirds, and bees.

Other Uses False rosemary is an excellent choice for homeowners seeking drought-tolerant, low-maintenance plants for their landscapes. It can also live in a terracotta pot in well-drained potting mix.

Coreopsis lanceolata
Lanceleaf Coreopsis

Say: kor-ee-OP-sis
lan-see-oh-LAY-tuh
Family: Asteraceae (Daisy)
Other names: Tickseed, coreopsis
Origin: Fields and glades in almost all of North America east of the Rockies

Zones: 3–8
Light: Sun to partial shade
Water use zone: Moderate to low
Size: 12 to 24 inches tall
Soil: Slightly moist, well-drained
Salt tolerance: Moderate

Lanceleaf coreopsis has masses of one- to two-inch, bright yellow flowers. It is a good selection if a groundcover is needed for harsh conditions such as roadsides and pond banks. This fast-growing, long-blooming perennial wildflower is commonly found in glades, sandy open ground, and along roadsides throughout much of the United States. Foliage is evergreen in most of the South. The tendency of the plants to form clumps with most of the foliage concentrated at the base makes it an excellent groundcover selection.

Right Place Choose a place in full sun with slightly moist, well-drained soil. Plant seeds in a garden or meadow from October through January. Plant about one-eighth of an inch deep in a firm seedbed that has been cleared of competing plants. Order seeds that were grown in your area for best results.

Continued Care Irrigate a coreopsis seed bed occasionally during dry winters until plants are well established. If fertilizer is used, apply a low rate of controlled-release fertilizer. Remove spent flowers for continued bloom. In late fall some plants may die from diseases, but since they reseed, very little loss is noticeable in an established planting. Mow in late fall or early winter, if desired.

Propagation *Coreopsis lanceolata* can be started from division or by seeds. Divide in late winter or early spring. Collect seeds soon after they ripen, because seedheads shatter easily. Dry seeds thoroughly and store in the refrigerator until planting time.

Kinds Several species of coreopsis are native to the South. Among the perennial species are *Coreopsis auriculata* (dwarf-eared coreopsis), *C. grandiflora* (bigflower coreopsis), *C. rosea* (rose coreopsis), and *C. verticillata* (threadleaf coreopsis). *C. tinctoria* and *C. basalis* are annuals. In addition to the species, many cultivars are available.

Value to Wildlife Coreopsis seeds are a favorite food of goldfinches and other seed-eating birds.

Gaillardia pulchella
Blanket Flower

Say: gay-LAR-dee-uh pul-KEL-uh
Family: Asteraceae (Daisy)
Other names: Indian blanket, firewheel
Origin: Indigenous to the Southwest but found eastward to Florida and throughout the eastern and central U.S.

Zones: 8–10
Light: Sun
Water use zone: Low
Size: 18 to 24 inches tall by 12 inches wide
Soil: Well-drained
Salt tolerance: High

Brilliant daisylike flowers adorn blanket flowers throughout the summer. Single, semidouble, or double flowers are held well above the foliage. They may be red, orange, yellow, or bicolors. Gray-green leaves are soft and hairy.

Right Place Plant seeds of blanket flower in fall or early winter at the rate of ten pounds per acre, or one ounce per 272 square feet. Scatter seeds on well-drained soil in full sun, and cover with one-eighth inch of soil. For the home landscape, place container-grown plants 12 to 15 inches apart after danger of frost is past. Plant in full sun and well-drained soil.

Continued Care Water regularly in the absence of rain until seeds germinate. Once established, plants are drought tolerant and carefree if planted in well-drained soil and full sun. Deadhead to prolong flowering. In spring, thin plants to the desired spacing if too many come up. Remove old plants periodically to allow new, more vigorous plants to grow.

Propagation *Gaillardia pulchella* is a reseeding annual or short-lived perennial. Once established, it will reseed for many years. Dried seed-heads can be collected from existing stands.

Kinds More than two dozen species of *Gaillardia* exist, most of which are native to North America. 'Yellow Sun' and 'Red Plume' are cultivars of *Gaillardia pulchella*. Several hybrid blanket flowers claim *G. pulchella* as a parent. *G. x grandiflora* is a cross between *G. pulchella* and *G. aristata*. Cultivars of the cross are 'Goblin', 'Sundance Bicolor', 'Tangerine', 'Burgundy', and many others. These hybrids reseed, but the offspring differ from the original plant.

Value to Wildlife Nectar is consumed by butterflies, and seeds are eaten by birds.

Other Uses Blanket flower blooms well on coastal beach-front property or sand dune reclamation sites. It is often planted on roadsides, drainage ditch slopes, open fields, and meadows. Gaillardia makes an excellent addition to borders and beds. It is a popular cut flower and lasts about a week in a vase.

Helianthus debilis subsp. *debilis*

Beach Sunflower

Say: heel-ee-ANTH-us DEB-bil-liss
Family: Asteraceae (Daisy)
Other names: Dune sunflower
Origin: Southeastern Texas to
Florida's east coast
Zones: 8–11

Light: Sun
Water use zone: Low
Size: 18 inches by 2 to 4 feet wide
Soil: Adaptable, well-drained
Salt tolerance: High

Beach sunflower is a perennial groundcover in frost-free areas. In areas with freezing winter temperatures, it is a reseeding annual that behaves like a perennial. Expect it to grow about 18 inches tall and spread by underground runners to cover an area about two feet square.

Yellow, slightly nodding, daisylike flowers with purplish-brown center disks bloom throughout the year in frost-free areas. Sand-papery, heart-shaped leaves that are two to four inches long and almost twice as wide offer the perfect backdrop for the sunny flowers.

Right Place Beach sunflower appreciates a place in full sun with well-drained soil.

Continued Care Occasional irrigation along the beach front might be beneficial, but over irrigation in other locations can slow growth and cause the plants to decline. Plant these beauties in a place where water from the sprinkler system does not reach. One light fertilization might encourage plants to cover quickly, but be sure to use a light hand; none is better than too much. No pests seem to bother beach sunflower.

Propagation Seeds or softwood cuttings can be used to propagate beach sunflower. Seeds are produced prolifically and sprout readily where they fall. Seedlings can be removed and planted in other places.

Kinds There are at least 150 species of sunflowers, including *Helianthus annuus,* the giant sunflower from which we get seed and oil; and *H. tuberosum,* the roots of which form Jerusalem artichokes. Authorities recognize two forms of *H. debilis.* One is the prostrate *H. debilis* subsp. *debilis.* The other is *H. debilis* subsp. *cucumerifolius* (Cucumber-leaf sunflower) which is erect and grows four or five feet tall.

Value to Wildlife Beach sunflower is attractive to butterflies, other pollinating insects, and birds.

Other Uses Floral designers enjoy beach sunflower in floral designs and in cut bouquets. It makes an excellent addition to butterfly gardens and is a plant of choice for dune plantings and walkways along the beach.

Heartleaf Wild Ginger

Say: hex-uh-STY-lus
  air-ih-FOH-lee-uh
Family: Aristolochiaceae (Birthwort)
Other names: Little brown jug, wild
  ginger
Origin: Southeastern North America
  from Virginia to Louisiana

Zones: 6–8
Light: Sun to partial shade
Water use zone: Moderate to low
Size: 6 to 12 inches
Soil: Acid, well-drained, woodsy soil
Salt tolerance: Slight to none

Heartleaf wild ginger with its evergreen, glossy, triangular, five- to eight-inch leaves is perfect for woodsy sites in small gardens. For groundcover use, it does not make a thick carpet, but spreads loosely to form a clump about 18 inches in diameter.

In spring, interesting purplish-brown blooms hug the ground. These "little brown jugs" often go unnoticed since they are sometimes covered by leaf litter.

Right Place The native range is pine woods, hardwoods, and swamp forests in very acid to acid, rich, moist to dry, well-drained soil in shade to half shade.

Continued Care Grow wild ginger in a shady place under trees or in front of taller plants. Their leaves will burn in sun. No other care is needed except to keep more vigorous species from displacing it.

Propagation Divide in fall and transplant to permanent locations. Collect seeds after they ripen in mid to late summer and sow on the surface of the soil in pots. Cover lightly with a layer of sand, and leave them outside over winter. Seeds should germinate the following spring.

Kinds Sometimes heartleaf wild ginger is called *Asarum arifolium.* Scientists have assigned the deciduous wild gingers to the *Asarum* genus, and evergreen species are assigned to the genus *Hexastylis.* Varieties of evergreen gingers include *H. arifolia* var. *arifolia, H. arifolia* var. *callifolia,* and *H. arifolia* var. *ruthii.* Very close examination (usually by scientist under a microscope) is required to determine the differences.

Value to Wildlife Heartleaf wild ginger provides winter browse for white-tailed deer. Flowers are fertilized by beetles, gnats, flies, and other ground-feeding insects. Like other members of the birthwort family, they host larvae of the pipevine swallowtail butterfly.

Other Uses Some American Indian tribes used the roots of wild ginger medicinally as treatment for stomach ailments, heart trouble, backaches, whooping cough, and asthma.

Juniperus horizontalis
Creeping Juniper

Say: jew-NIP-er-us hor-ih-zon-TAL-is
Family: Cupressaceae (Cypress)
Other names: Trailing juniper, creeping cedar
Origin: Northern North America south to New Jersey
Zones: 4–9

Light: Sun
Water use zone: Low
Size: 1 foot tall by 10 feet wide
Soil: Alkaline to acidic, dry, sandy
Salt tolerance: High

Creeping juniper forms a dense, evergreen mat of fine-textured, plumelike foliage and is probably the most popular type of groundcover juniper. Long, flexible branches have needle-like, sharp-pointed leaves on new shoots, while older branches have elliptic, scale-like leaves. In cold months, foliage turns a purplish to mauve color. Plants are dioecious (separate male and female plants).

Right Place Plant creeping juniper in full sun. It is adaptable to most soils, including alkaline to acid, and heavy to sandy.

Continued Care Trim to control spread if necessary. Prune young growth to encourage branching, but be aware that older growth will not produce new growth when pruned. Juniper blight can seriously affect creeping juniper, and spider mites may need to be controlled. Fertilize little, if at all, and water only during severe drought.

Propagation Notoriously difficult to start from seeds, creeping juniper is most often started from cuttings or by layering. Even so, several months may be required before roots are formed.

Kinds Many cultivars of creeping juniper are available in the trade. 'Wiltonii' (also known as 'Blue Rug') is probably the most popular. Intense silvery-blue foliage grows four to six inches tall. Other popular cultivars include 'Plumosa' (up to two feet tall), 'Blue Chip' (eight to ten inches tall with very blue summer foliage), and 'Glauca' (very flat and less than three inches tall). 'Bar Harbor' (one foot tall by six to eight feet wide) is very salt tolerant. With at least 60 cultivars from which to choose, gardeners can find one that fills almost any groundcover need.

Value to Wildlife Foliage and fruits are eaten by moose, deer, and many small mammals. Fruits are eaten and dispersed by birds.

Other Uses Tea made from the berry-like fruit was used by Native Americans to treat kidney diseases, colds, and sore throats. In the landscape, creeping juniper is effective cascading over walls, slopes, or hanging baskets.

Licania michauxii

Gopher Apple

Say: lye-KAY-nee-uh
    miss-SHOW-ee-eye
Family: Chrysobalanaceae
    (Cocoplum)
Other names: Ground oak
Origin: Pinelands, sand dunes and
    dry, sandy habitats in the south-
    ern United States

Zones: 8B–11
Light: Sun
Water use zone: Low
Size: 3 to 18 inches high and spread-
    ing
Soil: Well-drained, sandy; slightly
    alkaline to acidic
Salt tolerance: High

Right Place Gopher apple grows best in full sun on well-drained, sandy soils. Place it in your poorest, sunniest site. Extremely drought- and salt-tolerant, it is a good groundcover for areas near bodies of salt water.

Continued Care If gopher apple grows taller than is desired for a groundcover, it can be mowed occasionally. Otherwise almost no care is needed for this highly adaptable native plant.

Propagation Propagation is most easily accomplished by planting seeds. Cuttings do not root well, and from all accounts, it is difficult to transplant. However, I have successfully transplanted clumps with good roots attached.

Kinds Although I am aware of no cultivars of *Licania michauxii,* other species of *Licania* occur in the tropics, some of which grow to tree size. In California the sansapote fruit is harvested from *Licania platypus.*

Leaves of gopher apple are one and a half to four inches in length, and they resemble a narrow oak leaf. Primary stems grow deep underground and gradually spread to form a groundcover that is semi-evergreen in the upper reaches of Zone 8, but evergreen in Zones 9 and higher.

Gopher apple is highly visible along roadsides. A drive down I-10 or almost any country road in the Deep South will reveal masses that have been growing along the roadside for years.

Blooms are clusters of white flowers that appear in May and June. In fall a fruit is produced that is one to two inches long and resembles—you guessed it—a small oval-shaped apple that a gopher might eat.

Value to Wildlife Many mammals, including the gopher tortoise, seek out the fruit. Bees, flies, and other flying creatures use the flowers as a source of nectar.

Other Uses Gopher apple is one of the best soil stabilizers for poor, dry, sandy soils near the coast and along roadsides. Extremely deep roots and waxy leaves make it tolerant of fire, scorching sun, and intense drought.

Mitchella repens

Partridgeberry

Say: my-CHELL-uh REE-penz
Family: Rubiaceae (Madder)
Other names: Deer berry, checker-
berry, squaw vine, squawberry
Origin: Rich woods in the Eastern
half of the U.S.
Zones: 4A–9B
Light: Shade

Water use zone: Moderate
Size: 2 inches tall spreading to 1 foot
wide
Soil: Light, sandy to loamy, moist,
well-drained, acid to neutral
soils.
Salt tolerance: Slight

In late spring, two white, tubular, half-inch flowers bloom inside one calyx. Both flowers have one pistil and four stamens. In one flower the pistil is short and the stamens are long; in the other flower just the opposite is true. Therefore neither flower can fertilize itself—both flowers must be cross-pollinated by insects in order to get a single healthy berry.

Oval to heart-shaped leaves about half an inch across grow opposite each other on a whitish, trailing stem. Fruit is a bright red oval berry about one-fourth to three-eighths of an inch across that is edible.

Right Place The forest floor is the preferred site for partridgeberry. Plant about one foot apart in the shade of trees or shrubs in light, well-drained but moist soil.

Continued Care This delicate creeping vine needs little care. Usually no supplemental irrigation is needed, but if the leaves wilt dramatically and begin to wither on the vine, a little extra water may save the day.

Propagation Seeds germinate well if berries are given a three-month stratification in the refrigerator. After removing pulp from stratified seeds, sow them in damp sand. When seedlings are large enough to handle, pot them up. Plant out the following spring. Cuttings of naturally layered stems can be made in spring. Divisions transplant easily and grow quickly.

Kinds Partridgeberry is a native plant for which there are no known cultivars.

Value to Wildlife The berry is favored by ruffed grouse, partridges, and other game birds, as well as by skunks and white-footed mice. Many insects and small creatures are at home underneath this matted groundcover.

Other Uses American Indians used squaw vine (partridgeberry) during the final weeks of pregnancy to ease childbirth. Nursing mothers applied a lotion made from the leaves to relieve soreness in their breasts.

Muhlenbergia capillaris

Muhly Grass

Say: mew-len-BER-jee-uh
 kap-ih-LAIR-iss
Family: Poaceae (Grass)
Other names: Gulf muhly grass, mist
 grass, hairawn muhly, pink
 muhly grass
Origin: Wet prairies, savannahs, and
 upland pine forests of the southern United States

Zones: 7–10
Light: Sun to partial shade
Water use zone: Low
Size: 3 to 4 feet by 3 to 4 feet
Soil: Adaptable, almost any
Salt tolerance: High

Muhlenbergia capillaris is a clump-forming grass that has a stiff, upright growth habit. Though nondescript during part of the year, it makes up for it in fall when delicate rose-to-purple flowers rise above the foliage in a rosy mist that lasts for six to eight weeks. In winter after the seeds ripen, the wispy plumes turn a light buff color. It is native to moist pine barrens near the Atlantic coast of North and South Carolina, Florida, Georgia, and parts of Mississippi and Texas. Individual plants can get up to three to four feet tall and almost as wide.

Right Place Muhly grass is a tough native that is tolerant of drought and salt spray as well as wet conditions. Space 24 to 36 inches apart in full to part sun. It is recommended for Zones 7–10 but performance is not as good in the hotter areas of Zone 10.

Continued Care Maintenance is a simple matter. Cut the foliage nearly to the ground in late winter or early spring. Though extremely drought-tolerant, plants will grow better with regular supplemental water. No pests or diseases cause problems.

Propagation Muhly grass is easily started from seeds or from division of existing clumps.

Kinds Gulf muhly (*Muhlenbergia capillaris*) is native in much of the South. Other species are native to Mexico and western parts of the United States. Some of the most popular species are *M. dumosa* (Zones 8–10) or bamboo muhly; *M. lindheimeri* (Zones 7–9) with blue-green foliage and soft pink plumage; and *M. emersleyi* (Zones 6–10), or bull grass.

Value to Wildlife Muhly grass provides food, shelter, cover, and nest-building material for birds. It also provides food for grazing animals, nectar for pollinating insects, and seeds for ground-level foragers.

Other Uses Muhly grass is frequently used as a reclamation plant in natural areas, and also for cut flowers, borders, roadside plantings, and meadows.

Phlox divaricata
Woodland Phlox

Say: floks di-var-ih-KAY-tuh
Family: Polemoniaceae (Phlox)
Other names: Wild blue phlox, wild sweet William
Origin: Woodlands of the eastern two-thirds of North America
Zones: 3–9

Light: Partial shade
Water use zone: Moderate
Size: 12 to 18 inches, clumping
Soil: Humus-rich, well-drained
Salt tolerance: None

Native wild blue phlox is often found along streams and in open woods, but it is equally at home at the front of a flower border. It is evergreen in most of the South and spreads at a moderate rate by rhizomes.

In spring, delicate half-inch rosy-lavender to soft pink, five-petaled flowers are held on upright stems above the foliage. Cultivars have been selected with flowers that are bright purple, white, and all shades of pink. Pictured is my favorite cultivar, 'Louisiana Purple'. I hardly notice it until it blooms; then it upstages its compatriots.

Woodland phlox can be grown in sun if moisture is sufficient, but it will go dormant during a drought.

Right Place Woodland phlox is perfect for naturalizing at the base of large trees. It prefers moist, humus-rich, well-drained soil, morning sun, and afternoon shade. The shallow root system benefits from mulch.

Continued Care Cut off faded blossoms after spring bloom. Fertilize lightly after this annual trim.

Propagation Wild sweet William can be started from seeds or cuttings. Division of established clumps yields many new plants. Dig up a clump, divide it with a sharp implement, and plant divisions in prepared soil.

Kinds Several cultivars of wild blue phlox have been selected and are widely available at garden centers. These are some popular favorites: 'Clouds of Perfume' (ice-blue, fragrant flowers), 'Fullers White' (fragrant, pure white flowers), 'Laphammi' (lavender blue flowers), 'Louisiana Purple' (deep purple flowers), and x

'Chattahoochee' (a cross between woodland phlox and prairie phlox).

Value to Wildlife Woodland phlox is an important butterfly nectar plant and may host larvae of certain moths such as the spotted straw moth.

Other Uses The shallow root system and loose structure of the plants make woodland phlox a good choice for overplanting bulbs. They are also great for planting under deciduous trees where they will receive sun during the winter and early spring and be shaded during the summer.

Phlox subulata

Moss Phlox

Say: floks sub-yoo-LAY-tuh
Family: Polemoniaceae (Phlox)
Other names: Creeping phlox, ground pink, thrift
Origin: Eastern United States
Zones: 3–9
Light: Sun

Water use zone: Moderate to low
Size: 3 to 6 inches tall by 18 to 24 inches wide
Soil: Sandy, well-drained
Salt tolerance: Slight

Moss phlox is a prostrate, mat-forming, evergreen perennial that grows three to six inches tall and spreads by stolons to cover an area 18 to 24 inches wide.

Although moss phlox looks quite needle-like, it is actually a soft green cushion during most of the year. For about four weeks in spring it is completely covered with small flowers in shades of white, pink, rose, lavender, or red. The most commonly seen color is a loud pink. Although I have tried many of the more subtly colored cultivars, this loud pink phlox is the best performing of the lot in my garden.

Right Place Moss pinks appreciate a sunny spot in well-drained, rather poor soil. Add a light application of slow-release fertilizer around the plants at planting time. Mulch with an organic mulch and water well until the soil is completely moist.

Continued Care Moss phlox appreciates a light application of fertilizer each spring. Water weekly during dry weather, preferably while the ground is still wet with dew. If foliage remains wet over extended periods of time, crown rot may occur. Growth is best if divided every three or four years. Watch for and treat for spider mites if necessary.

Propagation Divide plants in fall or winter. Take stem cuttings in summer and stick several in a container, or simply stick them where you want them to grow.

Kinds Many cultivars of *Phlox subulata* are available in shades of white, lavender, pink, rose, and red. Other perennial species are *Phlox pilosa* (downy phlox), *Phlox divaricata* (woodland phlox), *Phlox stolonifera* (creeping phlox), and *Phlox paniculata* (summer phlox). *Phlox drummondii* is a seed-grown annual.

Value to Wildlife Flowers are visited by butterflies and other pollinating insects.

Other Uses Moss phlox is great at the edge of a border or cascading down a container or wall. Perhaps its best use is in rock gardens since it is compact and creeps over rocks and edgings.

Serenoa repens
Saw Palmetto

Say: sair-ren-NOE-uh REE-penz
Family: Aracaceae (Palm)
Other names: None
Origin: Coastal plain from South Carolina to Louisiana
Zones: 8–11
Light: Sun to shade

Water use zone: Low (drought tolerant, but can also tolerate moist soils)
Size: 5 to 10 feet tall by 4 to 10 feet wide
Soil: Tolerant of most
Salt tolerance: High

Saw palmetto, named for the saw-toothed edges of the stems, has fan-shaped leaves held out from a central clump. Multiple trunks can creep along the ground and create a dense groundcover. Extreme sturdiness and salt tolerance make it a great asset in natural and seaside landscapes. Attractive flowers and berries add to the decorative impact.

Right Place Saw palmetto grows well in most soils in full sun to shade. Plant container-grown specimens on three- to five-foot centers for mass planting. Do not remove plants growing in the wild, for they do not transplant well.

Continued Care Water well until established, and then leave saw palmetto to its own devices. Occasionally remove the lowest dead limbs if they become unattractive.

Propagation Although saw palmetto does not transplant well, it is easily started from seeds. Sow seeds as soon as they are ripe. Pot up seedlings in individual pots and grow in a protected place for two winters. After that, they can be planted in a permanent place in the landscape.

Kinds Two forms of saw palmetto are recognized. The most common form is yellow-green in color. Less widespread is a variety with blue-green or silvery foliage which is sometimes referred to as *Serenoa repens* var. *glauca*.

Value to Wildlife Bees use the flower nectar to make a high-grade honey. The plants are host to the monk or Cuban skipper, the palmetto arpo skipper, and the palmetto-borer moth. Saw palmetto provides cover for wildlife, and the fruit is eaten by several bird species and by raccoons and other mammals.

Other Uses All parts of saw palmetto are used to treat a variety of human ailments, including prostate cancer, thyroid deficiencies, bronchitis, asthma, colds, urinary tract disorders, and other maladies.

Saw palmetto is a favorite material of floral designers. The palm heart or terminal bud is edible.

Sisyrinchium angustifolium
Blue-eyed Grass

Say: sis-ee-RINK-ee-um
an-gus-tee-FOH-lee-um
Family: Iridaceae (Iris)
Other names: Eastern blue-eyed
grass, stout blue-eyed grass, and
narrow-leaf blue-eyed grass
Origin: Eastern half of the United
States and Canada

Zones: 4–9
Light: Sun to partial shade
Water use zone: High to moderate
Size: 6 to 12 inches tall, slowly
spreading
Soil: Moist, well-drained, ordinary
garden soil
Salt tolerance: Slight

Sisyrinchium angustifolium is one
of about 75 species of
Sisyrinchium native to the
Western hemisphere. It is an
herbaceous, clump-forming,
perennial member of the iris family that grows in tufts of flat,
grasslike foliage. Clusters of star-
shaped flowers of blue, violet, or
white, bloom in spring.

Grasslike leaves might easily
be mistaken for a clump of grass
if not for the yellow-centered
flowers. Clumps can be found
growing naturally in wet prairies
and fields.

Right Place Plant blue-eyed grass in
full to part sun in moist, well-drained
ordinary garden soil.

Continued Care Divide in early
spring or fall every two to three years
to maintain vigorous, healthy plants.
Remove unwanted seedlings or transplant them to another place. Prune in
late spring to remove old flower heads
and seedpods, and again in autumn to
remove faded summer foliage.

Propagation Seeds are best sown as
soon as they are ripe, but spring-
planted seeds also germinate successfully. Seedlings volunteer around
established plantings. Division of
existing clumps in spring yields
many new plants.

Kinds Evidently this genus of plants
is hard to classify, for many synonyms of *S. angustifolium* exist (31
synonyms are listed on the Atlas of
Florida Vascular Plants that is maintained by the Institute for Systematic
Botany at the University of South

Florida). The most commonly used
synonyms seem to be *Sisyrinchium
bermudiana, S. gramineum,* and *S.
gramnoides.* The cultivar 'Lucerne'
has lavender blue flowers.

Value to Wildlife Bees and bee
flies visit the flowers to collect pollen
or suck nectar. Seeds are eaten by
prairie chickens, wild turkeys, and
songbirds.

Other Uses Use blue-eyed grass in
rock gardens, cottage gardens, border fronts, and along pathways.
Combine it with other low-growing
groundcovers such as dwarf sedum
or creeping thyme. Infusions have
been used to treat diarrhea, to regu-
late the bowels, and to treat stomach
worms.

Stokesia laevis
Stoke's Aster

Say: sto-KEE-see-uh LEE-vis
Family: Asteraceae (Daisy)
Other names: Stokesia
Origin: Southeastern United States
Zones: 5 (with protection)–10
Light: Sun

Water use zone: Moderate
Size: 12 to 24 inches tall by 12 inches wide
Soil: Well-drained, moist
Salt tolerance: Moderate

Stoke's aster is an evergreen perennial. In spring and early summer, shaggy, cornflower-like flowers bloom on erect stems held well above the basal rosette of foliage. Leaves persist in winter in dark green, attractive rosettes.

Right Place Plant stokesia in full sun to partial shade in well-drained soil. Protection from hot afternoon sun is beneficial. Set plants 9 to 12 inches apart and mulch with three inches of organic mulch. A light application of organic fertilizer added to the planting hole will be beneficial.

Continued Care Cut off spent flowers to promote more bloom. Trim off old foliage in early spring if it becomes unattractive during the winter. Apply a light application of organic fertilizer to the top of the soil in early spring and renew mulch if needed. Water during periods of drought, or weekly in the absence of rainfall. Divide clumps every three years to maintain vigor.

Propagation Division of clumps is the most frequent means of propagation, but seeds can be stratified for six weeks at 40°F and then planted in moist soil. Germination may take several weeks.

Kinds *Stokesia laevis* is the only member of its genus. However, a number of cultivars are available. 'Blue Danube' has five-inch flowers, 'Alba' and 'Silver Moon' have white flowers, and 'Mary Gregory' sports yellow blossoms. 'Omega Skyrocket' grows three to four feet tall and has pale blue flowers. Choose 'Rosea' if rosy-pink flowers are desired, and 'Wyoming' for its dark blue flowers. 'Bluestone' is a dwarf cultivar that grows up to ten inches tall. Other cultivars can be found with varying characteristics.

Value to Wildlife Stokesia is visited by butterflies.

Other Uses Plant Stoke's aster at the foreground of perennial beds and borders, or use it as a border plant along walkways or beds. Cut flowers are useful in bouquets and floral designs and last a week or more in the vase.

Tradescantia ohiensis
Spiderwort

Say: trad-es-KAN-tee-uh
  oh-high-EN-sis
Family: Commelinaceae (Spiderwort)
Other names: Bluejacket, snotweed
Origin: Native to Southeastern
  United States
Zones: 5–10

Light: Sun to partial shade
Water use zone: Low
Size: 1 to 3 feet tall and wide
Soil: Not particular
Salt tolerance: Moderate to low

Tradescantia ohiensis is a clumping herbaceous perennial that can be found growing in most of the southeastern United States. Three-petaled, one-inch flowers with yellow stamens grow tightly clustered at the tips of smooth, leafy stems. Blossoms are attractive in morning but often shrivel by afternoon. Flower color varies from magenta, blue, lavender, and rose to near white. Color variations can result from the alkalinity of the soil and from genetic differences of the plants. Narrow grasslike leaves up to one and one-half feet long and one and three-fourths inches wide clasp the stems. Stems are creased along the center rib, forming a channel or groove. Spiderwort has been called snotweed because of the mucilaginous, stringy substance that appears when stems are broken.

Right Place Plant spiderwort in sun to part shade in almost any place. Preference is for well-drained moist, acidic, sandy soil, but it is tolerant of drought and can withstand periodic flooding. Plants self-sow and are considered aggressive by some gardeners, so give them a place where this tendency will be an asset. Plants die down in winter, so take this into consideration when placing them in the garden.

Continued Care Cut back in mid-summer to encourage new growth and fall bloom. Divide clumps when they become too crowded.

Propagation Sow seeds in fall or divide clumps for additional plants.

Kinds Several species of *Tradescantia* are native to North and South America. The genus includes the popular but nonnative groundcover *T. pallida* as well as the invasive *T. fluminensis,* or white-flowered wandering Jew.

Value to Wildlife Heavy pollen and nectar production makes spiderwort flowers attractive to bees and butterflies.

Other Uses Use spiderwort in borders, naturalized areas, meadows, or open spaces of woodland gardens and along roadsides. Spiderwort can detect nuclear radiation. Stamen hairs on a plant change from blue to pink in proportion to the amount of radiation received. Several sources indicate that spiderwort is edible.

Zamia pumila syn. Z. floridana
Coontie

Say: ZAM-ee-uh pu-MIL-uh
Family: Zamiaceae (Cycad)
Other names: Florida arrowroot,
    Seminole bread
Origin: Native to Florida, West
    Indies, Central and South
    America
Zones: 8B–11

Light: Partial shade
Water use zone: Low
Size: 2 to 4 feet tall, 3 to 5 feet wide
Soil: Alkaline to acid; loam or sand
Salt tolerance: High

Coontie is an evergreen, palmlike perennial shrub that has fine textured, leathery, fernlike foliage. Blooms appear in spring followed by elongated fruit (cones) three to six inches long. Seeds are covered with red or orange-red flesh. Male and female reproductive parts are on separate plants.

Ability to pull its stem into the earth keeps it safe from fire and predation by herbivores. Large storage roots yield an edible starch, a characteristic that earned it the name Seminole bread. Coontie is actually a cycad, a group of plants that was once the dominant vegetation on earth.

Right Place Coontie adapts to a wide range of soil. Space 36 to 60 inches apart for groundcover use. Performance is best in some shade. Salt tolerance allows it to be planted near, but not directly on, the beach.

Continued Care Though pests are usually not a problem, Florida red scale, which may be fatal, must be controlled. Other problems include sooty mold, mealy bugs, and other scale. Plants that are too large or that are infested with scale can be cut back to the ground to produce new foliage. Once established, Coontie is very drought tolerant.

Propagation Coontie is difficult to transplant because of long tap roots. Seeds are slow to germinate, and seedlings grow very slowly.

Kinds *Zamia pumila* has many synonyms, such as *Zamia floridana, Z. angustifolia, Z. integrifolia,* and

about 42 others. There appears to be a wide-leafed form and a narrow-leafed form.

Value to Wildlife Beetles and small bees pollinate these plants. Seeds provide food for mockingbirds, blue jays, and many other birds as well as insects and small mammals. Butterfly larvae feed on the leaflets.

Other Uses Coontie is effective in mass plantings or can be used as a border or accent. It is also quite happy in pots, urns, or other containers either indoors or outdoors. Native Americans ground coontie roots into flour after the poisonous compounds had been removed.

Chapter 5

Herbs as Groundcovers

Madalene Hill and Gwen Barclay, in their book *Southern Herb Growing*, define an herb as "any plant that is cultivated or harvested for an interesting or unusual quality." I embrace that definition, as well. Some people, however, believe that an herb is an essentially unattractive plant that must be grown in its own area—maybe out back in the herb garden. Many are surprised to learn that scores of herbs are attractive in and of themselves and merit a place out front among the stars of the ornamental garden. Likewise, many others are well-suited for groundcover use in any area of the garden where their needs can be met.

Oregano

Allium tuberosum

Garlic Chives

Say: AL-ee-um too-ber-OH-sum
Family: Alliaceae (Allium)
Other names: Chinese chives,
  Chinese garlic, Chinese leeks
Origin: Southeast Asia
Zones: 4–8

Light: Sun to partial shade
Water use zone: Moderate
Size: 12 to 15 inches (foliage) 2 to 3
  feet (in flower)
Soil: Well-drained
Salt tolerance: Slight

Right Place Plant garlic chives in full to part sun in well-drained, fertile ground. Although they are drought tolerant, they thrive in moderately moist soil.

Continued Care To keep garlic chives from coming up in unwanted places, pick the flowers and toss them into your salads. Divide every three or four years to keep clumps vigorous. Fertilize with slow-release fertilizer in spring.

Propagation Usually garlic chives are propagated by division of established clumps every three to four years. They also self-sow and may become invasive in the garden if seed heads are not removed before they fall to the ground.

Kinds A mauve-flowered variety is available in the trade, as well as several cultivars, but the white-flowered variety is the most frequently encountered.

Other Uses Garlic chives can be

Garlic chives are grown for their flavorful leaves and flowers. Unlike onions and other kinds of garlic, the tough, fibrous bulb is not eaten. Leaves are flat and grasslike and not hollow like onion chives.

Garlic chives are equally at home in the herb garden and the flower border. Attractive flower clusters composed of many small, creamy white, star-shaped flowers stand well above the foliage on sturdy stalks in fall.

Garlic chives may get killed to the ground during the cold winter months but will return reliably in spring.

grown in the vegetable garden or flower bed. They make excellent edging along a mixed border or along a path. Fresh flowers are long-lasting in floral designs. Seed heads can be dried to make handsome additions to dried floral designs. Several medicinal properties have been attributed to garlic chives, including antibacterial, cardiac, digestive, and stomachic.

The sweet and garlicky flavor of garlic chives adds a distinctive flavor to soups, stir fries, and egg and fish dishes. Like onion chives, they can be chopped and sprinkled over potatoes and gravies. Leaves and flowers make tasty additions to salads.

Myrtus communis 'Compacta'
Dwarf Greek Myrtle

Say: MER-tis KOM-yoo-nis
Family: Myrtaceae (Myrtle)
Other names: Sweet myrtle, bride's myrtle
Origin: Western Asia and Afghanistan
Zones: 8–10

Light: Sun to partial shade
Water use zone: Low
Size: 2 feet
Soil: Well-drained, sandy
Salt tolerance: High

Dwarf Greek myrtle is an evergreen shrub with dark green, fragrant leaves. Creamy white flowers about one-half inch across bloom in the spring. Flowers are followed by berries that are purplish-black at maturity and are similar in size and shape to blueberries.

Right Place Greek myrtle grows best in full sun to light shade. It is heat, drought, and salt tolerant. Place in an area where the foliage remains as dry as possible. Soil must be well drained, or the plants will be susceptible to root rot.

Continued Care Trim Greek myrtle as desired to maintain size and shape. Watch for scale insects and spider mites. Treat if necessary.

Propagation Tip cuttings root well when placed in a damp planting medium. Seeds can also be planted.

Kinds Some species of Greek myrtle can become small trees, but plants are most often pruned to maintain a height of five to six feet.

'Microphylla', or narrow-leaf myrtle is slow-growing, and matures a little larger than 'Compacta'. *Myrtus communis* 'Boetica', or twisted myrtle has an interesting trunk and branching pattern and can grow into a 9 to 12 foot tree.

Other Uses Dwarf Greek myrtle is a favorite plant in coastal landscapes, and it is frequently a bonsai or topiary subject. Since Victorian times, it has been a favorite plant for knot gardens. It grows well in patio planters and pots and is sometimes used as a small hedge.

Flavor is somewhat like a mixture of bay leaf and rosemary. Sprigs tossed on the grill give foods an herby, smoky flavor. Use Greek myrtle to flavor chicken, fish, or pork. Fresh tender leaves are excellent with squash and zucchini, and vinegars infused with the leaves are flavorful. The small berries that follow the flowers can be used like juniper berries to flavor roast meats or marinades. Medicinally, parts of the plant have been used to treat ulcers, asthma, bronchitis, acne, hemorrhoids, and oily skin, among other ailments.

Origanum spp.

Oregano

Say: or-RI-ga-num
Family: Lamiaceae (Mint)
Other names: Creeping or prostrate oregano
Origin: Mediterranean Europe and Asia

Zones: 4–9
Light: Sun to partial shade
Water use zone: Low
Size: 18 to 24 inches by 2 to 3 feet
Soil: Well-drained, neutral to alkaline
Salt tolerance: Slight to none

The most popular oregano grown as a seasoning herb is Greek oregano (*Origanum vulgare* subsp. *hirtum*). Hairy leaves, intense flavor, and white flowers help to distinguish it from the others. Also very flavorful are Syrian oregano (*O. maru*) and Kyrgyzstan oregano (*O. tyttanthum*).

For groundcover use, other species are preferable, for the true Greek oregano becomes woody after two or three years and needs to be divided or replaced. Groundcover oregano tolerates moderate foot traffic, competes successfully with weeds, and lasts for years.

Right Place Well-drained, neutral to alkaline soil and full sun to partial shade are preferred. Plant about 15 to 18 inches apart out of the range of an automatic irrigation system so that foliage stays as dry as possible.

Continued Care Water sparingly. Large areas can be mowed or sheared back once every two weeks in summer to maintain a neat appearance. Fertilize lightly in early spring. Avoid extensive foot traffic.

Propagation Oregano is easily started from seeds, but they do not come true. The best way to get the oregano you want is to take cuttings or divide existing clumps.

Kinds Several species of oregano make excellent groundcovers. Creeping oregano (*O. vulgare humile*) is brilliant green. Creeping golden marjoram (*O. vulgare aureum*) is golden green in spring and fall and dark green in summer. Mounding marjoram (*O. marjorana* 'Betty Rollins') and Rosenkuppel oregano (*O. laevigatum*) both have dark green leaves. Others are listed in catalogs and on-line sources.

Other Uses Oregano is grown for ornamental, culinary, and medicinal uses. Use anywhere a low-growing groundcover is needed, or place in hanging baskets or other containers to cascade over the edges.

Culinary oreganos go well with rice and tomato dishes, salads, casseroles, soups, sauces, and poultry dishes. It is the classic pizza herb.

Poliomintha longiflora

Mexican Oregano

Say: po-lee-oh-MIN-tha lon-jee-FLO-ruh

Family: Lamiaceae (Mint)

Other names: Poliomintha, rosemary mint

Origin: Mexico and southwestern United States

Zones: 8–10

Light: Sun

Water use zone: Low

Size: 2–3 feet

Soil: Well-drained

Salt tolerance: Unknown

Although branches of poliomintha can grow up to four feet long, the plants do not get that tall in the landscape. Branches are lax and lie close to the ground. Mexican oregano is an evergreen shrubby perennial that blooms summer through fall with tubular pink to lavender flowers that the hummingbirds enjoy.

Right Place Plant masses of this tough plant in an area with lots of sun, and where its trailing habit is an advantage. Do not use it for a groundcover if you want a flat, even effect, for limbs of Mexican oregano will tumble over each other and create a wavy, undulating groundcover. While Mexican oregano is tolerant of the humidity of the Coastal South, it is intolerant of consistently wet soil.

Continued Care Cut back rangy limbs if needed, and prune in early spring before the growing season to remove any unsightly branches that were damaged by winter's cold. Little to no fertilizer is needed for good growth, and pests and diseases are not problematic if plants are correctly placed in the landscape.

Propagation Cuttings can be taken at almost any time of the year. Layering branches that lie on the ground is easy. Simply scrape or wound the underside of a branch and place it in contact with the soil by pinning it down or weighting it down with a rock or brick.

Kinds *Lippia graveolens* and *Monarda fistulosa* var. *menthifolia* are both called Mexican oregano. Like *Poliomintha longiflora,* however, they are not members of the *Origanum* genus.

Other Uses Mexican oregano is a natural to hang over low walls or drape from raised beds or containers. It attracts butterflies, bees, and other pollinating insects.

Use as you would oregano, but be a bit sparing, as it packs more flavor than garden oregano. In Mexico it is used to flavor beans and stews. Sprigs can be tossed on the grill before grilling steaks, and leaves are a flavorful addition to chicken marinades and stews.

Prostrate Rosemary

Say: rose-ma-REE-nus oh-fiss-ih-NAH-liss prost-RAY-tus

Family: Lamiaceae (Mint)

Other names: Creeping or trailing rosemary

Origin: Southern Europe to western Asia

Zones: 8B–10

Light: Sun

Water use zone: Low

Size: 10 inches to 2 feet tall; upright or spreading

Soil: Neutral to mildly alkaline

Salt tolerance: High

'Prostratus' is a low, spreading form of rosemary that is often used as a groundcover. Dark green, needle-like leaves contrast attractively with pale, silvery-gray young stems. Dense foliage forms a thick carpet. Lilac blue flowers bloom from the axils of the leaves along most of the shoot in early spring, and the whole plant is highly aromatic. Rosemary is not amenable to foot traffic.

Right Place Rosemary prefers full sun and well-drained, sweet soil (slightly alkaline). Avoid places where the foliage will be wet for long periods of time. Add sand or gravel to heavy clay soils to enhance drainage. Lime can be added to the soil if existing soil is too acid. Rosemary is an excellent choice for gardeners who live by bodies of salt water, for it is tolerant of salt spray.

Continued Care Prune as soon as flowers fade. Cut shoots back about two-thirds to keep plants compact. Plants are very drought tolerant once established. Fertilize lightly with all-purpose, slow-release fertilizer in spring.

Propagation Softwood cuttings taken in spring or semihardwood cuttings taken in summer root quickly in sand.

Layering is a dependable means of increase. Seeds take a long time to germinate and are often not like the parent.

Kinds Rosemary is available in a wide array of cultivars. Plants can be upright or spreading and may bear white, blue, or lavender flowers on plants from six inches to six feet tall. Some hybrids have gold or golden-edged foliage. Cultivars 'Salem' and 'Arp' are more winter hardy than other selections.

Other Uses Prostrate rosemary is effective planted on retaining walls and banks and is attractive in containers and hanging baskets. It is included in most herb gardens, for it has both culinary and medicinal uses.

Use rosemary to season many meats, especially pork, lamb, and venison. Add a bit to flavor sauces, barbeques, and biscuits.

Santolina rosmarinifolia

Green Santolina

Say: san-toh-LEE-na
  rose-ma-ree-nee-FOH-lee-uh
Family: Asteraceae (Daisy)
Other names: Lavender cotton, rose-
  mary santolina
Origin: Mediterranean area of Europe
Zones: 7–10

Light: Sun
Water use zone: Low
Size: 18 to 24 inches tall, spreading
  to 3 feet wide
Soil: Well-drained, nutrient poor
Salt tolerance: Moderate

Rosemary santolina is an ever-green shrub that grows to about two feet tall when in bloom and spreads to about three feet wide. It can be used as a groundcover in areas without any foot traffic. Yellow buttonlike flowers about half an inch in diameter bloom in summer.

Right Place Green santolina prefers a place in full sun and light, sandy soil. Drainage must be excellent. Once established it is very drought tolerant. Rich soil is not necessary, and very little if any fertilizer is required. It is quite hardy, and toler-ates temperatures down to 0°F as well as hot, direct sun.

Continued Care Green santolina tends to become open centered. This can be prevented by shearing the plants in early spring before growth begins. Either give it a light shearing or cut it back to a few inches high. Cut the flower stalks off after flower-ing.

Propagation Either seeds or cuttings can be used to start new plants. Seeds should be sown in flats or pots in early spring. Cuttings of half-ripe side shoots three to four inches long can be taken in midsummer and placed in moist, freely-draining pot-ting medium. Roots should form within two weeks.

Layering is easily accomplished by scarring the bottom of a branch and covering it with soil. After roots form, the branch can be detached and planted.

Kinds Several species of *Santolina* are in the trade, including *Santolina chamaecyparissus,* and *S. ericoides* (synonym *S. pinnata).* Cultivars of each species have been selected for certain characteristics. In addition, *Santolina rosmarinifolia subsp. ros-marinifolia* is available as well as several cultivars. Green santolina is sometimes listed by its synonym, *Santolina virens.*

Other Uses Santolina makes a low, formal hedge and a satisfactory edg-ing plant. Needle-like leaves are well-suited to topiary. Although not edible, pleasantly scented leaves repel moths, and yellow flowers can be cooked into a bright yellow dye.

Satureja montana
Winter Savory

Say: sa-tu-REE-ja mon-TAY-nuh
Family: Lamiaceae (Mint)
Other names: None
Origin: Italy
Zones: 5–11

Light: Sun
Water use zone: Moderate to low
Size: 1 to 2 feet
Soil: Well-drained
Salt tolerance: Unknown

Winter savory is a dark green, semi-woody, herbaceous perennial. Tiny white to lilac flowers typical of the mint family bloom on terminal spikes in mid to late summer, but they are frequently pruned before they bloom to promote fresh leaves for herbal uses.

Right Place Give winter savory at least six hours of sun a day and well-drained soil. Space about 18 inches apart for groundcover use.

Continued Care Cut back in spring to encourage compact growth. The longer the stems grow, the woodier they get. Frequent pruning encourages the growth of tender, more flavorful young stems. Remove old branches back to the ground once or twice a year to keep plants clean and to promote air movement. Fertilizer needs are very low, and no serious insects or diseases seem to bother winter savory.

Propagation Plants can be started from seeds, but they germinate slowly. Cuttings can be taken in late spring, or plants can be divided in early spring.

Kinds *Satureja montana illyrica* is a low-growing version of winter savory that tops out at six inches. The cultivar 'Nana' grows about eight inches tall and makes a great evergreen groundcover. Summer savory (*Satureja hortensis*) is an annual that has naturalized in sections of North America. Some claim that it has a sweeter, more delicate aroma than does winter savory. However, summer savory does not grow well in the hot South.

Other Uses Winter savory is an attractive low-growing border plant. Its size makes it appropriate for rock gardens and small areas. It is easily clipped into formal shapes and is useful in knot gardens. Essential oils are used in the food and perfume industry. Bees and other insects are attracted to the flowers.

Winter savory is a great mixing herb that blends well with culinary oreganos, thymes, and basils. Sprinkle it in herb cheeses and sautés, and use it to flavor meat, fish, salads, soup, stew, and sausage. Leaves are used fresh or dried.

Germander

Say: TEW-kree-um kam-EE-drees
Family: Lamiaceae (Mint)
Other names: Wall germander
Origin: Europe and southwest Asia
Zones: 5–9
Light: Sun

Water use zone: Moderate
Size: 12 to 20 inches by 12 inches
Soil: Well-drained, neutral to slightly acidic
Salt tolerance: Slight

Two-lipped, deep pink to dark purple flowers characteristic of the mint family bloom in spring on terminal growth. Glossy evergreen leaves are simple and have serrated edges. Germander is a woody perennial or evergreen subshrub that forms clumps and makes an excellent formal groundcover. Numerous ascending and spreading stems form a dense mound of foliage.

Right Place Plant germander in average, well-drained soil and full sun. Rich soil is far less important than good drainage.

Continued Care Pinch or shear after flowering to maintain dense, compact growth. Fertilize infrequently to prevent long shoots of tender growth. Germander responds to rigid pruning and can be sheared to within six inches of the ground. Although pest problems seldom occur, plants are susceptible to mildew, leaf spot, rust, and mites.

Propagation Take cuttings from early to midsummer. Seeds can be sown as soon as they are ripe and left to overwinter in a cold frame. Layering of low-hanging branches in spring will yield new plants.

Kinds *Teucrium lucidum* grows to two feet and has larger, gray-green leaves. *T. fruticans* is a tender perennial often grown in a container. *T.*

canadense is sometimes planted in hanging baskets where its creeping growth shows to best advantage. *T. marum* (cat thyme) is much loved by our feline friends. Several other species of germander are available for the collector.

Other Uses Germander is an excellent hedge material and is used in knot gardens and herb gardens. Blossoms provide nectar for bees and other insects. Floral designers enjoy making wreaths that serve as air fresheners. Sometimes germander is used in bonsai. Liqueurs, vermouths, and tonic wines owe some of their characteristic flavor to germander.

Germander was once used to facilitate weight loss, but then it was found to be hepatoxic, or cause liver problems. Formerly it was used for various medical problems, including gout. It was thought to protect against the poison of snakebite.

93

Creeping Thyme

Say: TY-mus ser-PIE-lum or
ser-PILL-um
Family: Lamiaceae (Mint)
Other names: Wild thyme, mother of
thyme
Origin: Northern Europe, Northern
Africa
Zones: 4–10

Light: Sun
Water use zone: Low
Size: 3 to 6 inches and spreading
Soil: Well-drained, neutral to basic
pH
Salt tolerance: Slight

Creeping thyme is a prostrate, mat-forming, evergreen perennial with tiny leaves. In spring small flowers in colors of pink, rosy purple, red, or white literally cover the plants. Place plants between stepping stones where fragrance will be released each time they are stepped on. Choose the thyme you need based on the length of stem between sets of leaves. Cultivars with the longest stem length between leaves spread the most; those with short spaces between the leaves stay quite compact.

Right Place Creeping thyme requires well-drained soil and a sunny location. Although rich soil is not necessary, growth will be best if poor soil is amended with organic matter. Soil tests may indicate a need to add lime.

Continued Care Although creeping thyme is drought tolerant, it will die out in a severe drought. Be sure that the soil is well-drained, but water during dry spells. Little if any fertilizer is needed, especially if organic matter was incorporated into the soil at planting time.

Propagation Seeds, divisions, layering, or cuttings will yield more plants. Seeds are very tiny and germination may be sporadic. Large divisions can be planted where they are to grow. Smaller divisions do best if planted in a container until established.

Kinds About 350 or more species are in the *Thymus* genus. Wooly thyme (*Thymus pseudolanuginosus*) is a useful groundcover. Growing less than one inch tall, it hugs the ground and produces few if any flowers. Many cultivars of *T. serpyllum* and *T. praecox* make choosing difficult. Taxonomically, the genus is very tricky, for the species hybridize freely with each other.

Other Uses Pollinating insects, especially bees, are attracted when thyme blooms. Small varieties grow well in cracks in walls and are often used as a groundcover for bonsai. Some medicinal uses are documented.

Thymus vulgaris (common thyme) is the most satisfactory thyme to grow for the kitchen. Use it in legumes, beef, lamb, pork, poultry, or leafy vegetables.

Tulbaghia violacea

Society Garlic

Say: Tul-BAG-ee-uh vy-oh-LAY-see-uh
Family: Amaryllidaceae (Amaryllis)
Other names: Wild garlic
Origin: South Africa
Zones: 7–10
Light: Sun to partial shade

Water use zone: Moderate
Size: 18 to 24 inches tall, moderately spreading
Soil: Well-drained, moderate fertility
Salt tolerance: Moderate

Society garlic sends up clusters of lavender, sweet-scented flowers from early summer through late autumn. Individual flowers start out being tubular but spread out at the tips into inch-wide, star-shaped flowers. Grasslike foliage grows about a foot tall and smells like garlic. The gardener wonders how it earned its common name. Flowers are attractive to bees, butterflies, and other pollinating insects.

Right Place Light to fertile, well-drained soil with adequate moisture gives the best performance. Although plants will grow in dry, sandy soil, they will not be as vigorous as those grown in better soil with adequate moisture. Flowering is best in full sun.

Continued Care For an attractive bed, remove spent flower stalks. Fertilize with slow-release fertilizer in spring. If foliage is damaged by cold temperature, cut it off at ground level.

Propagation Division of clumps offers the easiest means of propagation. Plants spread slowly and are not aggressive, but clumps can be divided every two or three years. Seeds can be planted, but it takes two or three years before they reach blooming size.

Kinds Several different species of *Tulbaghia* exist, and several cultivars of *T. violacea* can be found. The most common cultivars are 'Silver Lace' which has green leaves edged with white, and 'Variegata' which has a white stripe down the center of each leaf. 'Pearl' has white flowers and may be difficult to find. 'Tricolor' sports blue-gray, white-margined leaves and lilac-pink flowers.

Other Uses Crushed leaves repel fleas, ticks, and mosquitoes (and perhaps humans, as well) when rubbed on the skin. Plants are said to repel snakes and moles in the garden. This herb has been used to treat colds and coughs, pulmonary tuberculosis, and intestinal worms.

Flowers and foliage are edible and are frequently tossed into salads for flavor and color. Flowers are attractive decorating deviled eggs, stuffed celery, and other foods. The garlicky leaves can be used in soups as a garlic substitute.

Chapter 6

Some Groundcovers to Avoid or Use with Caution

For each exotic invasive groundcover, I have included information about how the Florida Exotic Pest Plant Council (FLEPPC) ranks each of these plants. Those that are in Category I are invasive exotics that are altering native plant communities by displacing native species, changing community structures or ecological functions, or hybridizing with natives. Category II is made up of invasive exotics that have increased in abundance or frequency but have not yet altered Florida plant communities to the extent shown by Category I species.

The University of Florida Institute of Food and Agricultural Sciences (IFAS) is assessing the status of non-native plants in Florida's natural areas. The list produced by this group is called the "IFAS Assessment." It lists plants that have been determined to be invasive and not recommended for different parts of Florida, as well as those that are not problem species and can therefore be recommended.

I have also noted other lists or authoritative sources on which the pest plants appear. I have not included the lists for individual states. Consult your Cooperative Extension Service or any one of several environmental agencies for a list of invasive plants that merit consideration in your state. In the interest of space, I have used the following acronyms in the text instead of the complete name of each entity. Both are listed below for reference.

HEAR	Hawaiian Ecosystems at Risk
N'EAST	Uva. R.J., Neal, & J.M. DiTomaso, 1997. **Weeds of the Northeast.**Cornell University Press, Ithaca, New York. 397 pp.
NE&GP	Stubbendieck, J., G.Y. Friisoe, & M.R. Bolick. 1994. **Weeds of Nebraska and the Great Plains**. Nebraska Department of Agriculture, Bureau of Plant Industry. Lincoln, Nebraska. 589pp.
PIER	Pacific Islands Ecosystems at Risk
SEEPPC	Southeast Exotic Pest Plant Council (A list of invasive plants from 13 southern states)
STATE	Assorted authors. 2005. **State Noxious Weed Lists for 45 States**. State agriculture or natural resource departments.
USFWS	The U.S. Fish and Wildlife Service list of "Invasive Plants in Our Backyards."
WI	Hoffman, R. & K. Kearns, eds. 1997. **Wisconsin Manual of Control Recommendations for Ecologically Invasive Plants**. Wisconsin Dept. of Natural Resources. Madison, Wisconsin. 102 pp.
WSWS	Whiteson, T.D. (ed.) et al. 1996. **Weeds of the West**. Western Society of Weed Science in cooperation with Cooperative Extension Services, University of Wyoming. Laramie, Wyoming. 630 pp.
WWIAS	100 of the World's Worst Invasive Alien Species (part of the Global Invasive Species Database).

See links to other sources of information on invasive species at the Global Invasive Species Database at http://www.issg.org/database/reference/sourcesTP.asp.

Ardisia crenata

Coral Ardisia

Say: ar-DIZ-ee-uh kre-NAY-tuh
Family: Myrsinaceae (Myrsine)
Other names: Coralberry, Christmas
    berry, Hilo holly, marlberry,
    ardisia
Size: 2 to 6 feet tall
Native range: Japan to northern India

Zones: 7–10
FLEPPC rank: Category I
IFAS Assessment: Invasive and not
    recommended for north and cen-
    tral Florida
Other lists: HEAR, PIER, USFWS

Coral ardisia grows from two to six feet tall and has dark green, glossy leaves, white or pinkish flowers, and clusters of showy scarlet berries. It grows well underneath trees in average to moist soil. One look at these attractive plants in full berry is enough to make most gardeners want to include them in their landscape. Education, however, is the answer to this problem. As gardeners learn to recognize exotic invasive species and become aware of their potential to harm natural areas, they are less likely to allow them in their gardens.

Ecological Threat Native plant species diversity is lower where coral ardisia is present. Light is reduced in forest understories. Native ground-covers such as violets and trilliums are eliminated by the closely spaced ardisia plants which grow as thickly as 100 plants per square meter. Plants quickly regrow from the base when they are cut down.

Methods of Reproduction and Dispersal Red berries are attractive to birds, particularly cedar waxwings and mockingbirds. Seeds germinate readily, have a high rate of germina-tion, and are viable for a long time. Loads of volunteer seedlings can be found around established plants.

Range Coral ardisia is naturalized on two islands in Hawaii. In Florida and Louisiana it has invaded natural areas in several places, and it has been reported in Texas where it dom-inates the understory in parts of two reserves.

Management Approaches In Gainesville, Florida, at Colclough Pond City Nature Park, ardisia and other invasives are treated with a low-volume basal herbicide applica-tion with Garlon 4 in JLB Oil (a ready-to-use basal oil that eliminates the need for diesel and kerosene). A red or blue dye is used to make iden-tification of treated stems easier. A 15% solution is sprayed as a basal bark treatment. Persistent removal of small infestations is effective.

Glechoma hederacea
Ground Ivy

Say: gle-KOH-muh
   hed-er-AYE-see-uh
Family: Lamiaceae (Mint)
Other names: Creeping Charlie, hay-
   maids, gill-over-the-ground

Origin: Europe
Zones: 5–9
FLEPPC rank: Not listed
Other lists: NE&GP, N'EAST, WI

Ecological Threat In natural habi-tats, ground ivy is very vigorous and can swamp smaller plants by forming dense patches that out-compete other plants for water and nutrients. In the landscape, it often falls from hanging baskets or escapes from areas where it has been planted as a groundcover.

Ground ivy continues to be sold at nurseries and on-line sources. Some sources describe it as "ram-pant" or "extremely vigorous." Various sources for the *Global Compendium of Weeds* list it in sev-eral ways, including weed, quaran-tine weed, noxious weed, garden escape, and environmental weed.

Methods of Reproduction and Dispersal Ground ivy spreads freely by the roots that form wherever stems touch the ground. Flowers pro-duce four nutlets each, which form new plants.

Ground ivy is problematic in many different situations, but is primarily a lawn weed. Small, round to kidney-shaped (rounded cordate), scalloped-edged leaves grow in profusion. Bluish-violet flowers bloom in spring. Although it thrives in shady areas where grass will not grow, it can also be a problem in full sun.

Ground ivy is most common-ly grown as an ornamental in hanging baskets, but it is also planted as a groundcover. The variegated form is particularly handsome. Reportedly, it is toxic to livestock. Medicinal uses include treatment for problems involving mucous membranes.

Range Ground ivy is common in moist grasslands and wooded areas, slopes, roadsides, railroads, and dis-turbed sites. It is found throughout the United States except for Hawaii, Nevada, New Mexico, and Arizona.

Management Approaches
Creeping Charlie is a weed in heavy, rich soils with high moisture content. If the infestation is small, control can be achieved through hand weeding. Repeated removal is necessary because the plant will continue to grow from any roots left in the soil.

If Creeping Charlie escapes into the lawn, consider using a product containing a systemic foliar herbi-cide that controls broadleaf weeds.

Hedera helix

English Ivy

Say: HED-dur-uh HEE-licks
Family: Araliaceae (Ginseng)
Other names: Ivy
Origin: Europe
Zones: 5–9
Size: To top of supporting structure

FLEPPC rank: Not listed
IFAS Assessment: Has been documented in undisturbed natural areas in northern Florida
Other lists: SEEPPC, STATE, WI

English ivy is a decorative, high-climbing evergreen vine with aerial rootlets which anchor it to almost any surface. Hundreds of cultivars exist, and most have leaves with three to five lobes. Leaves can be almost any shade of green or have yellow or white variegation. Juvenile growth is typically a non-reproductive groundcover. The mature form usually has leaves that are ovate to rhombic in shape, and it is during this stage that flowering and fruit production begins.

The American Ivy Society names a "Non-Invasive Ivy of the Year." The society maintains that the smaller and more variegated or the more deeply cut and delicate the leaves, the less invasive it will be.

Ecological Threat English ivy escapes from residential landscapes and invades forests and surrounding native landscapes to create what is called an "ivy desert." In an ivy desert, a forested area has English ivy wildly climbing up tree trunks and covering the canopy. Native ground-cover plants are absent because of the dense, thick mat of ivy ground-cover. It is host to bacterial leaf scorch (*Xylella fastidiosa*) that is harmful to many native trees, such as elms, oaks, and maples.

Methods of Reproduction and Dispersal English ivy reproduces vegetatively and by seeds. New plants grow easily from cuttings or where stems touch the ground. Seeds are dispersed primarily by birds.

Range English ivy occurs in at least 26 states, where it infests woodlands, forest edges, fields, hedgerows, coastal areas, salt marsh edges, and other upland areas.

Management Approaches A waxy cuticle gives the plant a high resistance to herbicide uptake. Non-selective herbicides are most effective in spring, during the time when tender growth is present. Persistent cutting with pruners or saws and pulling the plants from trees and the ground are effective. If vines are too thick to cut, one can strip the bark, notch it, and apply a dilute solution of herbicide.

Lonicera japonica
Japanese Honeysuckle

Say: luh-NIS-er-a juh-PON-ih-kuh
Family: Caprifoliaceae (Honeysuckle)
Other names: Hall's honeysuckle
Size: Rapidly spreading; unlimited
Native range: East Asia, including
   Japan and Korea
Zones: 5–10

Ecological Threat *Lonicera japonica* creates tangled thickets that invade fields, forest edges and openings, disturbed woods, and floodplains. It spreads rapidly and out-competes native vegetation for light and below-ground resources. Established vines can engulf small trees and shrubs and cause them to collapse under the weight. Few plants can grow beneath the dense canopy.

Management Approaches Since Japanese honeysuckle is evergreen and semi-evergreen, herbicides can be applied after native plants have become dormant. The most effective treatment is a foliar application of glyphosate herbicide (Roundup, Rodeo, or Accord) applied after native vegetation is dormant and when temperatures are near and preferably above freezing. Prescribed burns may be helpful. In areas with a small infestation, hand pulling is a viable option.

Range Japanese honeysuckle infests

FLEPPC rank: Category I
IFAS Assessment: Invasive and not
   recommended for Florida
Other lists: HEAR, N'EAST, SEEPPC,
   STATE, USFWS, WI, and others

Japanese honeysuckle is a perennial trailing or climbing vine. Leaves are evergreen in most of the South. Native honeysuckles are easy to distinguish from invasive honeysuckles by the upper leaves and berries. The uppermost pairs of leaves of *Lonicera japonica* are distinctly separate, while those of native honeysuckle are fused to form a single leaf through which the stem grows. Japanese honeysuckle has black berries, while our native honeysuckles have red to orange berries.

Fragrant white flowers that fade to yellow are borne in pairs. Its beauty lures uninformed gardeners to include it in their gardens.

natural areas throughout the southern states and beyond.

Methods of Reproduction and Dispersal Japanese honeysuckle spreads by seeds, underground rhizomes, and above-ground runners. It is a strong competitor because of wide seed dispersal (primarily by birds), rapid growth rate, wide habitat adaptability, its ability to capture resources both above and below ground, and because it has no natural enemies. Since it continues to grow throughout the winter, it has an unusually long growing season. Individual vines have numerous long runners which develop roots when the vines come in contact with the soil.

Lysimachia nummularia
Creeping Jenny

Say: ly-si-MAK-ee-uh num-ew-LAH-ree-uh
Family: Primulaceae (Primrose)
Other names: Moneywort, running Jenny, wandering Jenny
Size: Ground-hugging, 2 to 6 inches
Native range: Europe to Russia

Zones: 3–9
FLEPPC rank: Not listed
Other lists: HEAR, N'EAST, SEEPPC, WI

Ecological Threat Creeping Jenny invades floodplain forests, wet and mesic prairies, marshes, and swamps throughout its area. Plants tend to cover the ground with a dense mat of low-growing vegetation which excludes other herbaceous vegetation.

Methods of Reproduction and Dispersal Creeping Jenny is widely sold as an ornamental groundcover. It grows rapidly and spreads indefinitely, rooting at each node as it touches the ground. It also produces globose capsules that open to expose many seeds. It is a severe pest if allowed to escape into the lawn.

Range Creeping Jenny has escaped from places where it was cultivated in much of the United States and other temperate regions of the world.

Management Approaches Some control has been achieved by prescribed burning during a time when most other plants are dormant.

Creeping Jenny is a ground-hugging, evergreen vine that has been used as a groundcover in many places in the South. Small round, bright green glossy leaves are attractive, and during the summer this creeping relative of the primrose bears solitary, upturned cup-shaped flowers.

Sometimes it is used between stepping stones because it can tolerate some foot traffic. It is also attractive in hanging baskets, but pieces that break off can become established underneath. Because it is particularly vigorous in wet areas, it is sometimes recommended as a plant for bog or water gardens.

Creeping Jenny is available at many nurseries. The cultivar 'Aurea' has bright, yellow-green foliage and is attractive in the garden, especially when planted beside plants with dark-colored foliage. Although it is not as aggressive as the solid green form, it has been known to revert to the darker green of the species.

Hand-pulling is effective, but is not practical for large infestations. All stems and stem fragments must be removed. Treating with herbicides such as Roundup or Rodeo may be effective control measures. If creeping Jenny invades lawns, treatment with a broadleaf herbicide will help keep it under control.

Saponaria officinalis

Bouncing Bet

Say: sap-oh-NAIR-ee-uh
    oh-fiss-ih-NAH-liss
Family: Caryophyllaceae (Pink)
Other names: Soapwort, latherwort
Origin: Europe
Zones: 3–9

Ecological Threat Since bouncing bet grows into large, dense patches, it out-competes native species and decreases the plant diversity of an area.

Management Approaches In gardens, bouncing bet can be pulled several times a year. Pull after the plants have bolted but before seeds are produced, and repeat on any new shoots that arise. Alternatively, mow it several times a year. This practice will eventually deplete the nutrient reserves in the roots and lead to its demise. Cultural control involves preventing the establishment of new infestations by minimizing disturbance and seed dispersal and maintaining healthy native communities. According to the Cooperative Extension Service at Colorado State University, chemical herbicides containing sulfometuron and metsulfuron are effective if applied prior to or shortly after emergence.

Range The species has naturalized throughout much of North America,

FLEPPC rank: Not listed
Other lists: STATE, NE&GP, WSWS

Soapwort was brought to America from England by the colonists for its ornamental qualities and for its use as a cleansing agent. Since then it has spread throughout much of the country. Dense clusters of pale pink, fragrant flowers bloom from June through September. Plants reach a height of one to two feet and spread by rhizomes.

Saponins in the stems and roots of soapwort form a lathery soap when mixed with water. Since early days, it has been used as a cleanser for all manner of things, including the Shroud of Turin, priceless tapestries, and other items made of delicate fabrics. In addition, the plant has many medical applications, including its use as an expectorant, laxative, and diuretic.

The cultivar 'Flore-Pleno' has double flowers and is not as invasive as the species. However, the cultivar does not come true from seeds, so it should be deadheaded to prevent germination.

including Canada and Alaska. It is most often encountered in sandy soil along stream banks, roadsides, meadows, and waste places where the soil has been disturbed.

Methods of Reproduction and Dispersal The fruit of *Saponaria* is a many-seeded capsule which germinates easily. It also spreads by wide-ranging rhizomes.

Sphagneticola trilobata
Wedelia

Say: sfag-net-TEE-koh-luh
   try-lo-BAY-tuh
Family: Asteraceae (Daisy)
Other names: Trailing daisy,
   Singapore daisy, creeping ox-
   eye, yellow dots
Size: 10 to 14 inches tall, spreading

Native range: Central America
Zones: 8–11
FLEPPC rank: Category II
IFAS Assessment: Invasive and not
   recommended for Florida
Other lists: HEAR, PIER, WWIAS

Ecological Threat Wedelia easily escapes from gardens to roadsides and natural areas where it can out-compete native plants. A thick cover-ing develops that crowds out or pre-vents regeneration of other species. Ability to climb enables it to climb up through shrubs and trees.

Methods of Reproduction and Dispersal
Dumping of garden waste on vacant lots or uninfested areas is a common means of dispersal. Stems form new plants where they touch the ground, and cut pieces readily take root.

Range Wedelia has escaped cultiva-tion and established itself in native areas in three states, including Florida. Other areas of infestation include Hawaii, the Pacific Islands, Puerto Rico, and the Virgin Islands.

Management Approaches Control of large areas can be achieved by treating with an application of Roundup or other foliar herbicides, followed by additional treatments as needed. Small plantings can be dug,

Wedelia is a commonly used groundcover in the South. Attractive, deeply lobed, glossy leaves and a profusion of one-inch, yellow daisylike flowers entice gardeners to include it in their landscapes. As the plant creeps along the ground, it roots at the nodes and makes a dense, attractive groundcover.

Part of its allure is the fact that it grows almost anywhere with very little care. It is adapt-able to most soils and grows readily in sun or shade on moist to dry soils. In Zone 8 and in other areas were frosts occur, it may be killed to the ground in winter, but it returns reliably in spring. Wedelia is moderately salt tolerant and grows well at the seashore.

Be careful that wedelia does not escape into pasture land or where livestock grazes. It has been known to cause farm ani-mals to abort fetuses after they grazed on the plants.
Interestingly, this species has been used to treat hepatitis, indi-gestion, and infections.

placed in plastic bags until decom-position is complete, and then burned or discarded. Repeated attempts may be necessary for com-plete eradication.

Chapter 7

Annuals as Groundcovers

The use of annuals for groundcover is sometimes not considered in landscape design. This is unfortunate, for annuals can provide an almost never-ending variety of color and form that can be achieved with no other type of plant.

Annuals, generally speaking, are plants that grow, bloom, set seed, and die within one growing season. Biennials produce leafy growth one season and bloom and die the following season. Perennials usually last for three years or longer. However, the distinctions between these categories often become blurred. Some of our so-called annuals (begonias, impatiens, fan-flowers, pentas) are actually perennials in warmer climates or mild winters. Whether a plant falls within one or another of these categories is less important than the purpose for which it is grown.

Annuals require different treatment than other, more permanent ground-cover plantings. Dr. Jamie Gibson of the University of Florida recommends a "rip and replace" procedure for annuals used as groundcovers. Each season, masses of annuals are planted. After they finish blooming and begin looking tired, they are ripped up and replaced by another annual that will carry the color through the next season.

Many designers purposely leave a swath or strip of ground in which to plant seasonal annuals. Usually this area is planted twice yearly, once in spring and again in fall. This method of landscaping is popular in resort areas such as Destin, Florida, where masses of color are desired year-round, as well as in business and industrial settings.

Establishing a site for annual groundcover beds is much the same as for other types of plants. Because of the vigorous growth and high performance expectations of annuals in groundcover situations, proper bed preparation is crucial. Prepare the ground before plants are purchased. Dig the bed at least six inches deep. Incorporate two or three inches of organic matter into soil if it is too sandy or if it does not drain well.

Fertilize the bed at planting time, and plan to continue the fertilization program each month to maintain vigorous growth. A good rule of thumb is to apply 6-6-6 or a similar complete fertilizer at the rate of two pounds per 100 square feet of bed area at planting time. Each month sprinkle a bit more fertilizer into the bed area, or use foliar sprays every week or so. The use of controlled release fertilizers will lessen the need for repeat applications. Such fertilizers can be dug into the soil at planting time and applied on the surface of established plantings.

After beds are prepared, it is time to visit the nursery and select your plants. Look for healthy, quality plants. Buy several trays of whichever ones you select and plant them en masse for greatest color impact. Limit your choice to one or two colors to avoid a spotty effect.

Annuals for the South can be divided into cool-season and warm-season plants. Generally, cool-season plants are planted in late fall or early winter.

Many of them are colorful throughout the cool season. Some grow during the winter and give a burst of color in early spring until hot weather burns them out. For groundcover purposes, those that spend all season growing to blooming size are not the best choices for the rip and replace system. Neither are the reseeding annuals that are planted in fall for spring bloom, such as cornflower and larkspur. While these plants are desirable in home land-scapes, growing them in highly visible beds would mean that no color was evident for several months of the season.

The big three plant groups for dependable color during the winter are pansies (*Viola x wittrockiana*), violas (*Viola cornuta*), and ornamental cab-bages and kales (*Brassica oleracea*). They last throughout the winter and can be ripped up and replaced with summer annuals when the weather warms. Pansies and violas come in many colors, and cabbages and kales range from purple and pink to green and white.

Recently in trials conducted by Dr. Gibson at the University of Florida in Milton, colorful vegetables were grown for winter color. Proving useful in these trials were several different cultivars of *Brassica oleracea* (kale), includ-ing 'Red Bor', 'Winterbor', and 'Lacinato/Toscano'. *Brassica juncea* (mus-tards) that grew dependably were 'Red Giant', 'Osaka Purple', and 'Miike Giant'. Pak choi and Swiss chard, as well as a few other *Brassicas,* were also recommended for color in cool-season gardens.

Many annuals fill the bill for summer color. As long as annuals are not too tall, they can be used as groundcovers. Stunning combinations can be made by combining plants of contrasting colors, such as red salvia and yel-low marigolds, or white begonias and purple ornamental potatoes.

Below are some personal favorites. It is not intended to be a list of all annuals that could be used in the rip and replace scenario. Some plants need to be seen up close and personal to be appreciated, and some bloom for only part of the day. Annuals recommended for groundcover must hold their color over a long season and flaunt it boldly.

Ornamental pepper

Annuals for groundcover use

	Exposure
Ageratum houstonium (Ageratum)	S
Alternanthera ficoidea (Joseph's Coat)	S
Begonia semperflorens-cultorum (Wax Begonia)	S/PSh
Capsicum annuum (Ornamental Pepper)	S
Catharanthus roseus (Periwinkle)	S
Celosia plumosa (Celosia)	S
Gomphrena globosa (Globe Amaranth)	S
Impatiens walleriana (Impatiens)	Sh
Ipomoea batatas (Sweet Potato)	S/PSh
Pentas lanceolata (Egyptian Star Flower)	S
Melampodium paludosum (Melampodium)	S
Perilla frutescens (Perilla 'Magilla')	S/Sh
Salvia splendens (Pineapple Sage)	PSh
Scaevola aemula (Fanflower)	S/PSh
Senecio cineraria (Dusty Miller)	S/SH
Solenostemon scutellarioides (Coleus)	S/Sh
Tagetes spp. (Marigold)	S
Zinnia angustifolia (Narrow-leaf Zinnia)	S
Zinnia hybrida 'Profusion' (Profusion Zinnia)	S

Key: S = Sun   Sh = Shade   PSh = Part Shade

Color

Blue, purple, white

Foliage: lime green, burgundy, purple

pink, red, white, rose

green, yellow, orange, red

white, pink, red

plumes of red, pink, gold, or white

White, pink, purple

red, pink, coral, white and combinations

Dark purple, chartreuse, variegated

White, pink, lavender, red

Yellow

Magenta, pink, white; most intense coloration in full sun

red, purple, white, peach

Blue, purple, pink, white

Gray, silver

Wide variety of leaf shapes and colors

Yellow, gold

White, gold, yellow

Cherry, orange, white

Chapter 8
Other Plants Suitable for Groundcover Use

Any book which attempts to list all plants suitable for certain uses, such as groundcover, inevitably falls short of the mark becauses there are literally thousands of appropriate plants. Even as this book goes to press, I continue to notice or discover groundcovers that I wish could be included. An example is the beautiful plant pictured below. Surely, hundreds more exist that I know nothing about.

As with most undertakings, the more one studies and learns, the more one realizes how much more there is to know. This section on "Other Groundcovers" is my attempt to list briefly many other suitable groundcover plants. I list them with the knowledge that many are left out.

Veronica peduncularis 'Georgia Blue' is a vigorous groundcover that bears blue flowers in the spring. Evergreen foliage turns bronze during the winter months. It grows six inches tall and up to four feet across and is hardy in Zones 4–9.

Perennials

Unlike some of the other plants usually considered for groundcover use, perennials are often grown as much for their flowers as for their ability to cover the ground. Many, though not all of them, die down during the winter but reappear the following spring. Like all other plants, careful attention must be given to putting them in the right place in the landscape and providing all the elements necessary for them to thrive.

Armeria maritima

Sea thrift

Family: Plumbaginaceae (Leadwort)

Plant type: Herbaceous perennial

Flower/Fruit: Flower pink to white in spring

Size: 6 to 12 inches tall and wide

Exposure: Sun

Zones: 4–8

Origin: Europe

Salt tolerance: High

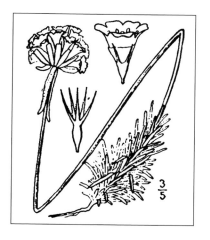

Plant sea thrift in dry, infertile, well-drained soil. It is not well suited to the moist humid regions of the South as the center tends to rot if foliage is not kept dry. A dense mass of stiff, grasslike foliage spreads slowly. This characteristic makes it a great choice for a small area, but impractical as a large scale groundcover. Plants tolerate salt spray.

Artemisia stelleriana 'Silver Brocade'

Dusty miller, beach wormwood

Family: Asteraceae (Daisy)

Plant type: Deciduous perennial

Flower/Fruit: Yellow showy flowers in summer

Size: 6 to 20 inches tall by 18 to 24 inches wide

Exposure: Sun

Zones: 3–9

Origin: Asia

Salt tolerance: High

Artemisia stelleriana 'Silver Brocade' has white to silvery feltlike lobed leaves. It is drought tolerant and needs little fertilizer. Do not allow leaves to stay wet any longer than necessary. Cut dead stems back to the crown in spring before new growth emerges.

Astilbe spp.

False spirea

Family: Saxifragaceae (Saxifrage)

Plant type: Flowering herbaceous clumping perennial

Flower/Fruit: Pink, red, crimson, purple, white blooms in late spring, early summer

Size: Varies with species and cultivar; from 6 to 36 inches tall

Exposure: Shade to partial shade

Zones: 6–8

Origin: Japan, Korea, China

Salt tolerance: Unknown

Astilbes are grown for their feathery plumes of flowers. They appreciate moist, well-drained, acidic soil that is rich in organic matter. Fertilize faithfully each season and divide every three to four years to maintain vigor. Select species and cultivars that bloom in early, mid, and late season for a succession of blooms. Just before new growth emerges in spring, remove the previous year's debris. Performance is best in the northern areas of its hardiness zone.

Bergenia cordifolia

Heartleaf bergenia

Family: Saxifragaceae (Saxifrage)

Plant type: Evergreen, clumping perennial

Flower/Fruit: Flower color ranges from deep pink to pale pink and occasionally white.

Size: 12 to 18 inches tall by 12 inches wide

Exposure: Partial shade

Zones: 4–10

Origin: Siberia

Salt tolerance: Moderate

Although bergenia has been cultivated in home gardens for over a century, the past hundred years or so have seen the development of many hybrid cultivars. Heartleaf bergenia spreads slowly by rhizomes. Three- to six-inch clusters of flowers appear in late winter or early spring. Although it is rated for zones 4–10, it seems poorly adapted for Florida and the Gulf Coast region. It appreciates rich, moist soil, and grows well in damp rocky woodlands and meadows.

Epimedium spp.

Barrenwort, horny goat weed, Bishop's cap

Family: Berberidaceae (Barberry)

Plant type: Herbaceous perennial

Flower/Fruit: White, cream, rose, lavender, or yellow flowers in spring

Size: 6 to 20 inches tall, depending on the species

Exposure: Shade to partial shade (more sun in moist soil)

Zones: 5–9

Origin: China

Salt tolerance: Unknown

Barrenwort needs soil with medium drainage and fertility but can survive in the dry, depleted soil beneath trees. New leaves are often a shade of coppery red. Plants grow at a slow to moderate rate by creeping underground stems. Shear in late winter to keep the planting neat, and feed in early spring with all-purpose fertilizer or compost. Propagate by division of clumps. The plants have been used in the treatment of liver and kidney ailments as well as for sexual dysfunction.

Gaultheria procumbens

Teaberry, creeping wintergreen, spice berry

Family: Ericaceae (Heath)

Plant type: Broadleaf evergreen shrublet

Flower/Fruit: White, bell-shaped blossom in spring; reddish edible berry

Size: 3 to 5 inches tall, spreading

Exposure: Shade to partial shade

Zones: 4–9

Origin: Eastern North America

Salt tolerance: Unknown

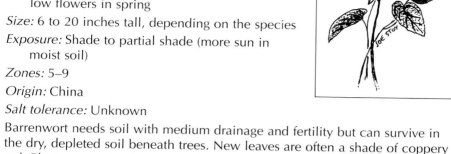

Leaves smell like wintergreen when crushed. Give plants a place in acidic soil and water regularly in the absence of rain. Teaberry spreads slowly by rhizomes to make an attractive groundcover. It is best in regions with cool summers, so folks in the Deep South will have less success than those in the upper regions of the South.

Heuchera spp.

Alumroot, coral bells

Family: Saxifragaceae (Saxifrage)

Plant type: Herbaceous clump-forming perennial

Flower/Fruit: Airy bell-shaped flowers rise above the foliage in spring

Size: Varies with species and cultivar

Exposure: Partial shade in the South; can take more sun in the northern part of its range.

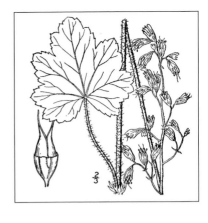

Zones: 4–9

Origin: USA and western Canada

Salt tolerance: Heuchera 'Purple Palace' is moderately salt tolerant. Others unknown.

Heuchera sanguinea is the species that produces the pink- and red-flowered coralbells. Other eastern species have led to hybrids that sport variously colored foliage, from purple to white to orange. *Heucheras* generally grow as tufts of foliage from which spikes of small flowers rise from spring to summer, and they vary in size from a few inches high to over three feet tall. Plant them in well-drained soil in light shade. Evergreen, colorful foliage is their main attraction.

Lamium maculatum

Spotted deadnettle

Family: Lamiaceae (Mint)

Plant type: Semi-evergreen, herbaceous perennial

Flower/Fruit: Small, pink, lavender or white, depending on cultivar

Size: 10 inches tall by 18 inches (or more) wide

Exposure: Shade to partial shade

Zones: 3–8

Origin: Europe and North America

Salt tolerance: Unknown

Spotted deadnettle needs evenly moist, well-drained but moderately fertile soil. The plant dies out in too much sun and cannot withstand drought. However, it makes a vigorous groundcover in moist, shaded areas and may even become invasive in places where its cultural needs are met. Attractive cultivars have variously colored leaves and include 'Beacon Silver', 'Cannon's Gold', 'Chequers', 'Pink Pewter', 'White Nancy' and others.

Laurentia fluviatilis syn. *Isotoma axilaris*

Blue star creeper

Family: Lobeliaceae (Lobelia)

Plant type: Evergreen, spreading groundcover

Flower/Fruit: Small blue flowers in late spring and summer

Size: 2 inches tall spreading to 18 inches wide

Exposure: Sun to partial shade

Zones: 5–10

Origin: Australia

Salt tolerance: Unknown

Blue star creeper seems to be well named, since it creeps slowly and has blue, star-shaped flowers over a long season. It grows well between stepping stones and even tolerates light foot traffic. Plant in well-drained but moist soil. Tiny green leaves form a dense carpet and are especially useful in baskets. Some gardeners have reported that their plants get a disease and die out after a period of time. Use a suitable fungicide, if necessary, to control this problem.

Mazus reptans

Creeping mazus

Family: Scrophulariaceae (Figwort)

Plant type: Creeping evergreen to semi evergreen perennial

Flower/Fruit: Flowers lavender with white and yellow markings in early summer

Size: 2 inches tall; spreads by creeping stems which root at the nodes.

Exposure: Sun to partial shade

Zones: 5–8

Origin: Himalayas

Salt tolerance: Unknown

Creeping mazus grows best, perhaps even too vigorously, in organically rich soil that is consistently damp but well drained. Narrow, bright green leaves form a dense carpet which remains evergreen in warm climates. Since it is tolerant of light foot traffic, it is ideal around stepping stones. Mow occasionally if needed.

Pulmonaria spp.

Lungwort

Family: Boraginaceae (Forget-me-not)

Plant type: Clumping mostly evergreen perennial

Flower/Fruit: Flowers may range from salmon to raspberry to sky blue

Size: Usually 6 to 10 inches tall; dependent upon species and cultivar

Exposure: Shade to partial shade

Zones: 4–9

Origin: Europe

Salt tolerance: Unknown

The lungworts appreciate well composted soil. Search out *Pulmonaria longifolia* and its cultivars 'Bertram Anderson', 'E.B. Anderson', 'Little Star' and others. This narrow-leafed species seems to perform better in the South than some of the others. Leaves are present for most of the winter but die down just before new ones emerge in the spring. Foliage colors vary from apple green through olive to a very dark green spotted with brilliant silver.

Sarcococca hookeriana var. *humilis*

Sweet box, Christmas box

Family: Buxaceae (Boxwood)

Plant type: Evergreen shrub with stoloniferous growth habit

Flower/Fruit: Fragrant white flowers in early spring; blue-black berries in summer

Size: 1 to 2 feet tall by 1.5 to 2.5 feet wide

Exposure: Partial shade

Zones: 5–8

Origin: Western China

Salt tolerance: Unknown

These plants need organically rich soil. Mature clumps produce suckers and reproduce along stolons, so they spread slowly to cover an area. Slim, pointed, glossy leaves are attractive year-round. Tiny sparklerlike flowers add a pleasing fragrance to the winter garden, and the berries that follow add to their attractiveness. Sometimes stems are cut for Christmas decoration.

Serissa foetida

Serissa, yellow rim, snow rose

Family: Rubiaceae (Madder)

Plant type: Small evergreen or semi-evergreen shrub

Flower/Fruit: Pink buds, white, funnel-shaped flowers from early spring until late fall

Size: 2 to 4 feet tall and wide; cultivars smaller

Exposure: Prefers morning sun and afternoon shade

Zones: 8–10

Origin: Southern China

Salt tolerance: None

Serissa is frequently used as a bonsai subject. It is amenable to pruning but intolerant of drought. Cuttings root easily. Plant in protected locations, as it may be severely damaged by frost. Several cultivars are available, some of which are variegated. The species name *foetida* means "stinking" because the roots emit a curious odor when they are disturbed.

Waldsteinia fragarioides

Barren strawberry

Family: Rosaceae (Rose)

Plant type: Evergreen perennial

Flower/Fruit: Bright yellow spring blooms

Size: 4 to 6 inches tall by 1 foot wide

Exposure: Shade or partial shade

Zones: 4–8

Origin: Eastern North America

Salt tolerance: Unknown

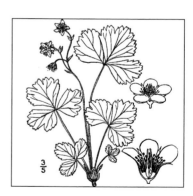

Barren strawberry tolerates the dry shade beneath trees, but it can also deal with some sun. Toothed, trifoliate (three leaflet) leaves resemble strawberries, and it propagates by stolons. *Waldsteinia fragarioides* is a good choice for the upper reaches of the South. *W. parviflora* is native from Virginia to Georgia and may be better adapted to warm climates.

Ferns

Many ferns can be used as groundcovers in the South. The partial list below names some of the most commonly selected ones. Most of these ferns naturalize readily, last for many years, and grow into lush groundcovers in woodland areas. Most are finely textured, so they contrast well with the bold, coarse-textured leaves of such plants as hosta, cast iron plant, and caladium.

Adiantum pedatum

Maidenhair fern

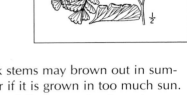

Family: Pteridaceae (Maidenhair fern)

Plant type: Native deciduous fern

Size: To 18 inches tall and 2 feet wide in 10 years

Soil: Moist but well-drained

Exposure: Shade

Zones: 3–8

Origin: United States

Salt tolerance: None

Light green, delicate-looking fronds with dark stems may brown out in summer if heat is intense and soil becomes dry or if it is grown in too much sun. This fern is best in shaded gardens, and is especially interesting in spring when the pink crosiers (fiddleheads) emerge.

Asplenium platyneuron

Ebony spleenwort

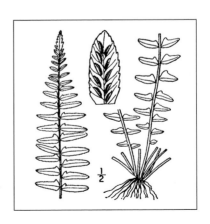

Family: Aspleniaceae (Spleenwort)

Plant type: Native evergreen fern

Size: To 20 inches tall and 12 inches wide

Soil: Medium-wet, well-drained soils, but can tolerate some drought

Exposure: Shade to part sun

Zones: 3–8

Origin: Eastern North America, South Africa

Salt tolerance: None

Best use of ebony spleenwort is in shady areas of rock gardens, native plant gardens, or woodland sites. Avoid overwatering and poorly drained areas, as crown rot may occur if the roots stay too wet. Stem is glossy, purplish- to red-brown. Fertile fronds grow upright, while the shorter, sterile fronds are more arching.

Athyrium goeringianum

Japanese painted fern

Family: Dryopteridaceae (Wood fern)

Plant type: Deciduous fern

Size: To 15 inches tall and wide

Soil: Moist; intolerant of drought

Exposure: Shade

Zones: 3–8

Origin: Japan

Salt tolerance: None

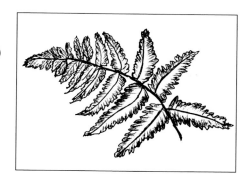

The cultivar 'Pictum' is frequently selected for its gray-green, silver, and purple variegated coloration.

Dennstaedtia punctilobula

Hay-scented fern

Family: Dennstaedtiaceae (Bracken fern)

Plant type: Native deciduous fern

Size: 2 to 3 feet tall and spreading

Soil: Adaptable to many conditions including salt spray and dry soil

Exposure: Part shade to sun

Zones: 3–8

Origin: United States

Salt tolerance: High

The scent of new-mown hay emanates from the bruised leaves of this fern. It is a tough, rapidly spreading, ground-covering fern.

Dryopteris ludoviciana

Southern shield fern

Family: Dryopteridaceae (Wood fern)

Plant type: Semi-evergreen clumping native fern

Size: To 3 feet tall and wide

Soil: Usually found in swamps, but adapts to normal garden conditions

Exposure: Shade to part sun

Zones: 6–9

Origin: Southeastern United States

Salt tolerance: None

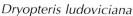

Upright form lends this fern to use as a specimen or as a groundcover in the garden.

Onoclea sensibilis

Sensitive fern or bead fern

Family: Dryopteridaceae (Wood fern)

Plant type: Native deciduous fern

Size: 12 to 24 inches tall and vigorously creeping

Soil: Best used in poorly-drained soils

Exposure: Sun to part shade

Zones: 3–8

Origin: Eastern United States

Salt tolerance: Unknown

Sterile fronds on separate stalks look like clusters of beads. Autumn color is yellow, and it dies down at the first hint of frost. In ideal conditions it may become a pest, but it is useful in poorly drained areas where other ferns would not prosper.

Sensitive fern is widely distributed in the United States, and inhabits wet meadows, riverbanks, swamps, and bogs from Manitoba to Newfoundland southward to Texas and the Gulf Coast.

Sensitive fern may be confused with *Woodwardia areolata*, but a quick glance will reveal that sensitive fern has pinnae (leaves attached to the stem or rachis) in opposite arrangement, while those of *Woodwardia* are alternate. In addition, the fertile fronds are very dissimilar (see illustrations).

Osmunda regalis

Royal fern

Family: Osmundaceae (Royal fern)

Plant type: Deciduous fern

Size: To 4 feet tall; clumping fern which spreads slowly from a central crown

Soil: Moist, water-retentive soil

Exposure: Shade to part shade

Zones: 3–10

Origin: Africa, Asia, Europe, North America, South America

Salt tolerance: Slight to none

In very wet places royal fern may grow up to six feet tall, but it grows shorter in a regular garden setting. Royal fern is threatened in Iowa, commercially exploited in Florida, and exploitably vulnerable in New York.

Phegopteris hexagonoptera

Broad beech fern

Family: Thelypteridaceae (Marsh fern)

Plant type: Deciduous native fern

Size: 18 to 24 inches tall and spreading by creeping rhizomes

Soil: Native garden soil unamended

Exposure: Shade

Zones: 5–9

Origin: Eastern North America

Salt tolerance: Unknown

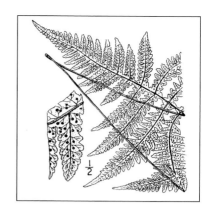

Named because of its association with American beech trees, this woodland species is widely distributed across the eastern United States. Too much sun causes it to die back, so be sure to plant it in deep shade. Although it is listed as a threatened plant in Minnesota, a plant of special concern in Maine, and exploitably vulnerable in New York, this fern can become invasive in good garden soil according to the Missouri Botanical Garden.

Polystichum acrostichoides

Christmas fern

Family: Dryopteridaceae (Wood fern)

Plant type: Native, nearly evergreen fern

Size: 18 to 24 inches tall and clumping

Soil: Damp, moisture-retentive soil

Exposure: Shade to part sun

Zones: 5–10

Origin: Eastern North America

Salt tolerance: None

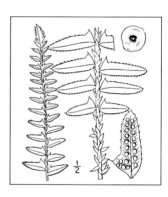

This well-behaved fern is found on stream banks, swamps, and other damp to wet places. It performs well in regular garden settings provided the soil is moisture retentive but well drained. Glossy, dark green fronds are popular in flower arrangements, especially around Christmastime when their evergreen fronds are easy to spot in the woods. When held upside down, the pinnae (leaves attached to the stem or rachis) look like little Christmas stockings, which may be the reason for its common name. Plants grow from a crown that will eventually make a large, dense clump. It is useful for combating soil erosion on slopes.

Thelypteris kunthii

Wood fern, Southern shield fern

Family: Thelypteridaceae (Marsh fern)

Plant type: Deciduous, fast-growing fern

Size: To 3 feet tall; rhizomatous clumps spread to make large masses.

Soil: Well-drained soil; drought tolerant

Exposure: Sun to part shade

Zones: 8–10

Origin: Southeastern United States

Salt tolerance: Slight

This yellow-green, fine-textured fern has large triangular fronds which contrast attractively with the straw-colored stems. Showy rhizomatous clumps spread to make attractive masses. Grow this fern if you need one that is tolerant of drought or that will grow in a sunny exposure.

Woodwardia areolata

Netted chain fern

Family: Blechnaceae (Chain fern)

Plant type: Native, deciduous fern

Size: 18 to 24 inches tall and spreading 12 to 18 inches wide

Soil: Medium to wet, organically rich

Exposure: Shade to part shade

Zones: 5–9

Origin: Eastern and Southern United States

Salt tolerance: Moderate to slight

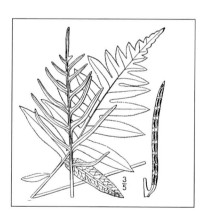

Netted chain fern remains compact and neat-looking in the landscape. Interesting, upright fertile fronds appear in fall. Plants spread by branching and creeping rhizomes and will naturalize over time into large colonies if growing conditions are favorable.

Casual observers will notice the close similarity of netted chain fern to sensitive fern. Distinguish between them by the fertile fronds, which are dissimilar (see illustrations). Also, the sterile fronds of netted chain fern have leaflets that are narrower and less lobed than those of sensitive fern.

Ferns that should be avoided

Lygodium microphyllum and *Lygodium japonicum*
Japanese climbing fern and old world climbing fern

Family: Lygodiaceae (Climbing fern)

Plant type: Climbing fern

Size: To the top of any support

Zones: 8–11

Origin: Old world tropics and subtropics; Japan

These two vinelike ferns are capable of smothering trees, fences, native groundcovers, and tree seedlings.

Sandra Murphy-Pak

Tectaria incisa
Incised halberd fern

Family: Dryopteridaceae (Wood fern)

Plant type: Invasive, evergreen fern

Size: To 35 inches tall and rapidly spreading

Zones: 9–11

Origin: New world tropics

This fern threatens to out-compete our native halberd fern, so it should never be planted in Florida and other areas where it is hardy.

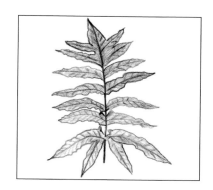

Nephrolepis cordifolia
Sword fern

Family: Dryopteridaceae (Wood fern)

Plant type: Evergreen fern hardy to 25°F; propagates mainly by spreading hairy runners

Size: 2 to 3 feet tall and spreading indefinitely

Zones: 6–10

Origin: Pantropical

If a sword fern in your landscape produces a tuber, remove it, for it is the invasive *N. cordi-*

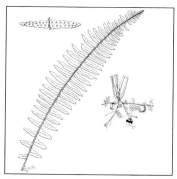

Anna Ramey

folia. An excellent comparison of the native sword ferns and the invasive sword fern can be found on the University of Florida website http://edis.ifas.ufl.edu. The title of the article by Dr. K. A. Langeland is "Natural Area Weeds: Distinguishing Native and Non-Native 'Boston Ferns' and 'Sword Ferns' (*Nephrolepis* spp.)."

Salvinia molesta and *Salvinia minima*

Floating fern and water fern

Family: Salviniaceae (Floating fern)

Plant type: Floating, rootless aquatic ferns

Size: A single plant can fill 40 square miles in 3 months; extremely invasive

Zones: 7–11

Origin: South America

Laura Line

These ferns grow exponentially and quickly fill the quiet water of lakes, ponds, ditches, and slow-flowing rivers and streams. Chances of purchasing *Salvinia molesta* at a nursery are very slim as it is prohibited by law in the United States. It can be introduced into a body of water by emptying of aquariums or by boats and other water craft or equipment. Like other invasive plants, it grows aggressively and crowds out native species. Large, floating mats are formed that take up oxygen and degrade the quality of water for other aquatic plants and organisms.

Neither of these noxious ferns should be used in water features or aquariums under any circumstances.

Asparagus densiflorus

Asparagus fern

Family: Liliaceae (Lily)

Plant type: Evergreen plant hardy to 24°F

Size: 12 to 24 inches tall and spreading to 3 feet; rapid growth

Zones: 7–10

Origin: South Africa

While not a fern, this asparagus is often treated as a fern. Care should be exercised in its use, because it has escaped into natural areas in Florida and Hawaii. Plants bear small white flowers in spring followed by red berries. Propagation is by division of clumps or from seeds.

Asparagus fern is readily obtained at nurseries throughout the South and is widely planted as a groundcover. It is a favorite of floral designers who use the frothy fronds to enhance floral designs.

Shrubs

When thinking of groundcovers, shrubs are sometimes not considered. Many shrubs are low-growing and do not spread as exuberantly as vines, some ferns, and other plants that spread by creeping rhizomes or root at nodes along their stems. Most shrubs are mannerly in their growth habits. Using some of the low-growing selections as groundcovers is a solid investment in long-lasting and easy-to-maintain parts of the landscape.

Abelia x *grandiflora* 'Prostrata'

Prostrate glossy abelia

Family: Caprifoliaceae (Honeysuckle)

Plant type: Evergreen shrub

Flower/Fruit: Clusters of fragrant white flowers in summer

Size: 1.5 to 2 feet tall; spreading to 4 or 5 feet

Exposure: Sun to partial shade

Zones: 6–9

Origin: China

Salt tolerance: Moderate to slight

Abelia prefers moist, well-drained soil, but is drought tolerant once established. It can be pruned severely. Glossy, dark green leaves of fine to medium texture turn bronze-green to bronze-red in winter.

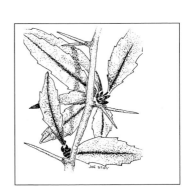

Berberis candidula

Paleleaf barberry

Family: Berberidaceae (Barberry)

Plant type: Evergreen shrub

Flower/Fruit: Bright yellow flowers in May and June. Very dainty and usually lost among the foliage. Fruit is a half-inch-long berry produced in fall.

Size: 2 to 4 feet tall; spreading to 5 feet wide

Exposure: Sun to partial shade

Zones: 5–8

Origin: China

Salt tolerance: Slight to none

Paleleaf barberry is a low-growing, dense, rounded shrub with rigidly arching branches covered with three-pronged spines. Leaves are dark green on top and pale green or whitish below. Often they turn bronze to wine-red in fall and winter. Plants withstand severe pruning. Some cultivars of *Berberis thunbergii* (Japanese barberry) are also used as groundcovers, but they sometimes do not tolerate the heat of Zone 8 as well as *B. candidula*.

123

Buxus microphylla

Littleleaf box, boxwood

Family: Buxaceae (Boxwood)

Plant type: Evergreen shrub

Flower/Fruit: Small flowers in spring, not showy, but fragrant and attractive to bees. Fruit is a shiny black three-celled capsule.

Size: Depends on cultivar

Exposure: Sun to partial shade

Zones: 6–9

Origin: Japan

Salt tolerance: Moderate

Since boxwood is shallow rooted, a good mulch should be applied to keep roots cool and moist. Cultivars 'Compacta', 'Morris Midget', 'Pincushion', 'Tide Hill', 'Winter Gem', and others are low-growing and well-suited for groundcover use. All cultivars accept pruning well and can be maintained at almost any height.

Grow littleleaf boxwood in average, medium wet, but well-drained soil. Protect from the extremes of winter weather as winter winds may cause the foliage to turn a bronze or yellowish brown color.

Buxus sempervirens

Common boxwood

Family: Buxaceae (Boxwood)

Plant type: Evergreen shrub

Flower/Fruit: Fragrant flowers in spring. Fruit is a three-horned capsule about a third of an inch long.

Size: Depends on cultivar

Exposure: Partial shade

Zones: 5–8

Origin: Southern Europe, northern Africa, western Asia

Salt tolerance: None

Root knot nematodes are problematic for common boxwood in the lower South and are best controlled by the liberal use of organic matter in the soil. Although some cultivars are treelike in habit, others grow much smaller and are suited for use as groundcovers.

'Suffruticosa' is a compact, very slow-growing cultivar that grows about two to three feet tall and wide in ten years. It can, however, be kept shorter with appropriate pruning. 'Vardar Valley' also tops out at two to three feet tall, but it grows as wide as three to six feet. This cultivar seems more resistant to leaf miner and mites than some of the others. 'Welleri' grows slowly to five feet tall, but like other cultivars, it can be maintained at a much shorter height.

Cotoneaster horizontalis

Rockspray cotoneaster

Family: Rosaceae (Rose)

Plant type: Evergreen shrub

Flower/Fruit: Pink-tinged flowers are showy when borne in abundance. Small, quarter-inch, bright red fruit are borne following the flowers.

Size: 2 to 3 feet tall; spreading 5 to 8 feet wide

Exposure: Sun to partial shade

Zones: 6–9

Origin: Western China

Salt tolerance: Slight to none

Rockspray cotoneaster prefers fertile, well-drained soil. Several cultivars are suitable for groundcover use. 'Little Gem' (also listed as 'Tom Thumb') is a dwarf form that grows to 12 inches tall. 'Perpusilla' grows to one foot tall and up to seven feet wide and is less susceptible to fireblight than some other cultivars. 'Saxatilis' is more compact than the species but fruits more sparsely. 'Variegatus' is a very slow-growing cultivar whose green and white leaves turn rose-red in autumn.

Other species of cotoneaster may also be suitable for groundcover use, but most are not well-suited to the South.

Danae racemosa

Alexandrian laurel, poet's laurel

Family: Liliaceae (Lily)

Plant type: Evergreen shrub

Flower/Fruit: White blooms are not showy. Half-inch cherry-tomato-red fruits in fall and early winter are very attractive.

Size: 2 to 4 feet tall and wide

Exposure: Shade

Zones: 7–10

Origin: Iran

Salt tolerance: None

Alexandrian laurel is suitable for shady sites and woodland gardens. It prefers moist, well-drained soil. The gracefully arching habit and lustrous, evergreen leaves make it attractive throughout the year. Floral designers use the long-lasting greenery in floral designs. No pests or disease problems are serious enough to cause concern. Alexandrian laurel is a relatively unknown plant, but it is worthy of much wider use in southern gardens. Plants are relatively expensive since it takes five to seven years for a plant to grow from seed into a saleable plant.

Native Plants

Homeowners will do well to look in the woods and uninhabited areas near their homes in their search for adaptable groundcovers. Most native plants have stood the test of time, are well-adapted, and grow easily in the garden. Many are coming out of the woods to assume starring roles in residential and commercial landscapes. Savvy nurserymen are beginning to catch on and propogate native plants to meet this growing market.

Aristida stricta

Wiregrass, pineland threeawn

Bloom time: Seedstalks occur only after a fire.

Flower color: Tan

Plant type: Densely tufted, perennial bunchgrass

Size: 18 to 36 inches tall and up to 6 inches across the base

Zones: 7–10

Light: Partial shade (as under pines)

Native habitat: Distributed on Atlantic coastal plain from southeastern North Carolina to southern Florida, and westward to Mississippi in areas maintained by fire

Salt tolerance: Unknown

Wiregrass is the primary grass cover in longleaf pine savannas and slash pine flatwoods. It is also found in wet areas, such as in pitcher plant bogs.

Chrysogonum virginianum

Green and gold

Bloom time: Spring, summer, fall

Flower color: Gold

Plant type: Evergreen herbaceous perennial

Size: 6 to 9 inches tall; spreading to 24 inches

Zones: 5–9

Light: Shade to partial shade.

Native habitat: Eastern United States

Salt tolerance: Unknown

Green and gold, a member of the daisy family, is listed as endangered in Kentucky and Pennsylvania and threatened in Ohio and Tennessee. This pretty native flower looks equally at home in the woods and in the flower garden. It is grown for its attractive, evergreen foliage and golden yellow daisylike flowers that bloom in spring and fall. It prefers moist, well-drained soil and can take limited foot traffic. Such attributes make it an excellent groundcover for woodland gardens or naturalized areas.

Dichondra carolinensis

Dichondra, kidney grass

Bloom time: NA

Flower color: NA

Plant type: Creeping prostrate evergreen
  perennial herb

Size: 2 to 3 inches tall; spread indeterminate

Zones: 8–9

Light: Sun

Native habitat: Carolinas

Salt tolerance: Low

Dichondra is sometimes used as a lawn substitute. It is also attractive in rock gardens where it is allowed to grow in and among the rocks. Almost no maintenance is required once it is established. Growth rate is rapid, and it can be mowed if desired. Kidney grass does not withstand foot traffic as well as lawn grasses. Some people take great pride in their dichondra lawn. Others consider it a lawn weed and do their best to get rid of it.

Eragrostis spectabilis

Purple love grass

Bloom time: Late summer, fall

Flower color: Purplish

Plant type: Grass

Size: 18 to 24 inches tall

Zones: 5–8

Light: Sun

Native habitat: Grows in fields and on roadsides in much of the United States.

Salt tolerance: Unknown

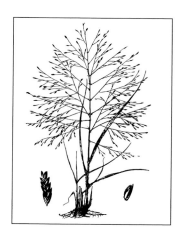

Plant drought-tolerant purple love grass in full sun in infertile, sandy soil. It spreads by rhizomes and can be propagated by seed or by division. Cut foliage to within a few inches of the ground in late winter before new growth begins. Purple love grass is attractive in perennial borders, as a specimen, and as groundcovers in open, woodland areas. Although it is native, it is listed as an invasive plant by the Nebraska Department of Agriculture where it is primarily a weed of pastures and hay-fields. However, it attracts butterflies and provides nesting cover for ground birds.

Ipomoea pes-caprae

Beach morning glory, railroad vine, bayhops

Bloom time: Summer

Flower color: Pinkish-purple

Plant type: Perennial vine

Size: Prostrate; 3 to 12 inches tall and spreading

Zones: 8–11

Light: Sun

Native habitat: Coastal beaches, dunes

Salt tolerance: High

Beach morning glory is a trailing vine that colonizes sand dunes. It establishes itself just above the high tide line and forms large mats with taproots that can penetrate more than a meter deep. These far-ranging roots are a first line of defense against the eroding effects of storms. Stems run along the ground and root at the nodes. Only the flowers are erect. Railroad vine likes full sun, is drought tolerant, and can tolerate the extreme heat, salt spray, and wave splash of coastal beaches. Bees, butterflies, moths, flies, beetles, wasps, and ants are pollinating insects that are attracted to the flowers. Seeds drift on the sea and germinate wherever they find a favorable site.

Mimosa strigillosa

Powderpuff

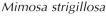

Bloom time: Late spring, early summer

Flower color: Pink

Plant type: Perennial vine, deciduous

Size: 6 to 12 inches tall and spreading

Zones: 8–11

Light: Sun

Native habitat: Moist, disturbed sites, stream banks, pinelands

Salt tolerance: Moderate

Foliage of the powderpuff is not freeze tolerant, but deep-reaching roots send up fresh foliage when winter is past. Sometimes used as a lawn substitute, it does well in areas without heavy foot traffic. Stems run along the soil surface, so it can be mowed with no detrimental effects. It is sometimes called sensitive plant because the leaves draw back when touched. This drought- and salt-tolerant native is attractive to bees and butterflies.

Pachysandra procumbens
Allegheny spurge
Bloom time: Spring
Flower color: Pinkish-white
Plant type: Perennial semi-evergreen groundcover
Size: 6 to 10 inches tall
Zones: 5–8
Light: Shade to partial shade
Native habitat: Rich woods in West Virginia down
    through Louisiana and across to Florida
Salt tolerance: None

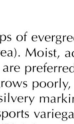

Allegheny spurge produces slowly expanding clumps of evergreen foliage
(semi-evergreen in northern reaches of hardiness area). Moist, acidic,
organic, well-drained soils and partial to full shade are preferred. Allegheny
spurge works great under shade trees where grass grows poorly, and it pre-
vents soil erosion on shady, sloping terrain. In fall, silvery markings appear on
the leaves. Cultivars include 'Eco Treasure', which sports variegated leaves;
'Forest Green', almost identical to the species; and 'Pixie', a miniature selection growing to four inches tall. This native species is a superior choice to its
Asian cousin, Japanese spurge *(Pachysandra terminalis)*, which spreads more
vigorously and aggressively.

Packera aurea
Golden ragwort, golden groundsel
Bloom time: Spring
Flower color: Yellow
Plant type: Perennial, evergreen
Size: 1 foot tall (2 feet when flowering)
Zones: 4–8
Light: Shade
Native habitat: Wet meadows, rich, moist
    woods, swamps, bogs
Salt tolerance: None

Golden ragwort is good for shady areas. It reseeds aggressively and also
spreads by stolons. Deadhead to prevent unwanted plants.

Phyla nodiflora

Capeweed, matchweed, turkey-tangle fogfruit (or frogfruit)

Bloom time: Spring, summer, early fall

Flower color: Pink and white

Plant type: Perennial, deciduous to evergreen

Size: 3 inches tall and spreading

Zones: 8–12

Light: Sun

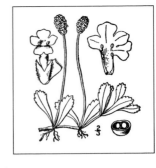

Native habitat: Moist sandy or rocky areas and beaches

Salt tolerance: High

Capeweed is a creeping/spreading, matlike groundcover sturdy enough to serve as a lawn substitute. In heavy traffic areas in full sun it is especially useful. Its best use is in natural areas well away from highly maintained lawns. PIER (Pacific Islands Ecosystems at Risk) considers it an aggressive weed that out competes other low-growing native species. Although it is able to withstand considerable drought, it looks better when given an occasional deep watering. Bees are attracted to the blossoms, so that might be a deterrent to using it in a children's play area. Butterfly enthusiasts usually have a patch of it because it is the host plant for Common Buckeye and Phaon Crescent butterflies.

Tiarella cordifolia

Foamflower

Bloom time: Spring

Flower color: Tiny white flowers above the foliage

Plant type: Clump-forming perennial that spreads by runners (stolons)

Size: 6 to 12 inches tall by 1 to 2 feet wide

Zones: 3–8

Light: Shade to partial shade

Native habitat: Nova Scotia south to Georgia

Salt tolerance: Unknown

Foamflower prefers moist soil that is high in organic matter. Leaf shapes and patterns are quite varied but look somewhat like a maple leaf. In spring, tiny white flowers with long stamens give the plants a frothy or foamy look and explain its common name. Leaves may have reddish veins and often turn a reddish-bronze in autumn and winter. Plants spread by rhizomes to form clumps one to two feet wide. Foamflower is evergreen in mild winters. It is a great groundcover for woodland gardens or moist areas such as stream banks.

Yucca filamentosa

Bear grass, Adam's needle

Bloom time: Spring, early summer

Flower color: White terminal raceme

Plant type: Evergreen perennial, basal clump of
tough, sword-shaped leaves

Size: Leaves to 2 feet tall; flowering stalk to 6 feet

Zones: 5–10

Light: Sun

Native habitat: Southeastern United States

Salt tolerance: High

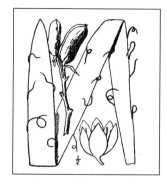

Some taxonomists recognize *Yucca filamentosa* as a separate species from *Y. smalliana, Y. flaccida*, and *Y. concava*, but others lump them together and treat them as a single species. Yucca prefers full sun and average to dry soil and is great for use in natural areas. Evergreen swordlike leaves one to three feet long and about an inch wide arise from a central rosette. Leaf margins are distinctive with fibrous white strands or filaments hanging from the sides of the younger leaves.

Bear grass is an effective groundcover even though the spectacular blooms may arise three to six feet above the foliage. Choose this as a ground-cover that directs traffic, since most people will walk around a mass planting of bear grass After flowering and fruiting the plant dies, but new plants grow from lateral buds that are produced by the mother plant.

Herbs

Many herbs make excellent groundcovers. Some have scented foliage and uses over and above their ornamental value. Some are edible, and many have medicinal applications. Crafters use herbs in wreaths, dried arrangements, potpourri, and for other decorative purposes. Herbs are popular for flavoring oils and vinegars. Fresh herbs are more aromatic and pungent than their dried counterparts. For some people, herbs will be included in the landscape because of these other uses.

Other gardeners, even if they do not capitalize on these alternative uses, find that the scents and textures of the herbs add another dimension to the landscape that makes time spent in the garden more enjoyable. Who among us has not bent to feel the wooly softness of lamb's ears? Who can walk by a patch of mint without snapping off a leaf to sniff or taste? Such characteristics earn herbs their place among other groundcovers.

Artemisia spp.

Mugwort, southernwood, tarragon, wormwood, artemisia, others

Say: ar-the-MEEZ-ee-uh

Family: Asteraceae (Daisy)

Origin: Varies with species

Zones: Varies; generally 5–9

Light: Sun

Water use zone: Low

Size: Varies with species and cultivar

Soil: Well-drained

Salt tolerance: Moderate

Artemisias are grown for their foliage effect in the garden. *Artemisia abrotanum* (southernwood), has finely divided, feathery textured leaves. *A. absinthium* 'Lambrook Silver' grows a bit tall for a groundcover, but can be trimmed during the summer to promote branching. *Artemisia* x 'Powis Castle' is a hybrid that is useful in many parts of the South. *Artemisia lactiflora,* or white mugwort, is the coarsest of the group, but it grows four to six feet tall and is most suited as a background plant. *Artemisia ludoviciana* (Louisiana artemisia) has such cultivars as 'Latiloba', 'Silver King', 'Silver Queen', and 'Valerie Finnis' that are excellent groundcovers. *Artemisia schmidtiana* 'Nana' or 'Silver Mound' is a popular and frequently used groundcover. *Artemisia stelleriana,* or beach wormwood, can also be used in mass plantings. The trick in growing most of these plants is to give them plenty of sun and to keep the soil lean and dry.

Centella asiatica

Gotu kola, Asiatic pennywort, coinwort

Say: sen-TELL-uh a-see-AT-ee-kuh

Family: Apiaceae (Parsley)

Origin: Asia

Zones: 7–11

Light: Sun

Water use zone: High

Size: 3 to 6 inches tall and spreading

Soil: Moist

Salt tolerance: Unknown

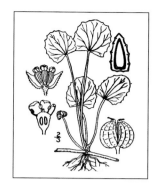

Gotu kola reproduces by producing new plants above-ground, and also spreads by underground rhizomes. It prefers wet, sandy soil enriched with organic matter. This plant, which has naturalized in many parts of the world, is one of the most important medicinal herbs. In Western medicine, it is used to improve circulation, to combat stress and depression, to heal wounds, and to treat many other maladies. It has medicinal uses throughout the world. It is an interesting groundcover plant for herb gardens and out-of-the-way places where it is confined to one area.

Galium odoratum

Sweet woodruff, sweet-scented bedstraw

Say: GAL-ee-um oh-dor-AY-tum

Family: Rubiaceae (Madder)

Origin: Eurasia, North Africa

Zones: 4–8

Light: Shade

Water use zone: High

Size: 6 to 12 inches tall and spreading

Soil: Rich, moisture retentive

Salt tolerance: Unknown

Sweet woodruff is a short to medium-size perennial groundcover with whorled leaves which
blooms with white flowers in late spring. It is capable of self sowing and spreads by creeping rhizomes. When grown in optimal conditions it can become invasive. In the lower reaches of the South, it usually melts out in the heat of summer.

Helichrysum angustifolium

Curry, immortelle

Say: hel-ih-KRY-sum an-gus-tee-FOH-lee-um

Family: Asteraceae (Daisy)

Origin: France

Zones: 8B-11

Light: Sun

Water use zone: Low

Size: 12 to 18 inches tall by 3 to 4 feet wide

Soil: Well-drained

Salt tolerance: Unknown

Essential oils have cooling and rejuvenating qualities that make it suitable for skin care preparations. The aroma of a curry powder is pervasive on warm southern air. Plant in the driest, most well-drained area you can manage, and leave space between plants for air circulation.

Mentha spp.

Peppermint, spearmint, apple mint, many others

Say: MEN-tha

Family: Lamiaceae (Mint)

Origin: Europe

Zones: 5–9

Light: Partial shade

Water use zone: Moderate

Size: Most are spreading groundcovers to 12 inches tall

Soil: Moisture retentive, fertile

Salt tolerance: Unknown

Mints are semi-prostrate, perennial herbs that are grown for their aromatic and flavorful foliage. They have square stems and opposite leaves. The invasive nature of most mints is understood by all who have ever added it to their gardens. To many, however, mint is an essential herb, and a place will be found. Preferably, the site will be contained by solid walls or other impediments that stop its rhizomes from spreading into unwanted areas. It is also good if it is in a place where it can be mowed to encourage new leaves. Species intermix freely. Stems can grow two to three feet high and small flowers are produced in late summer. Propagate by root divisions or stem cuttings. Avoid using manure on plantings because it may cause rust disease. Many species and hybrids are available, including peppermint, spearmint, curly mint, apple mint, pineapple, Corsican, pennyroyal, and others.

Stachys byzantina

Lamb's ears, wooly betony

Say: stack-iss biz-an-TEE-nuh

Family: Lamiaceae (Mint)

Origin: Turkey and Iran

Zones: 4–7

Light: Sun

Water use zone: Low

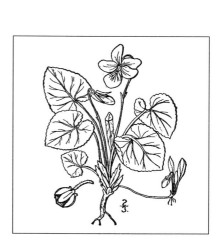

Size: 4 to 6 inches tall and 1 to 2 feet wide (before flowering)

Soil: Friable, well-drained, excellent drainage

Salt tolerance: Unknown

For groundcover use, find a dry, well-drained place in the landscape away from the reaches of the automatic irrigation system. Unfortunately, in Zones 8 and above it often falls victim to high humidity. Under ideal circumstances, and in climates with low humidity, lamb's ears form a mass of silvery foliage like a living carpet spread across the ground.

Viola odorata

Sweet violet

Say: vy-OH-luh oh-dor-AY-tuh

Family: Violaceae (Violet)

Origin: Europe

Zones: 4–9

Light: Shade

Water use zone: Moderate

Size: 6 to 12 inches tall and spreading

Soil: Almost any

Salt tolerance: Unknown

Sweet violets are now naturalized over much of the country. They spread by short runners and set copious seeds that come up wherever they fall. Flowers are small and range in color from deep purple or blue to pinkish or even whitish-yellow. All have five petals. Violets have many medicinal applications, and they are edible. Some gardeners consider them to be invasive.

Plants to Avoid or Use with Caution (refer to page 96)

Some plants grow more exuberantly than we would like them to in confined garden spaces. However, the plants in this section do far more than that. They escape cultivation, set up housekeeping in native areas, and upset the balance of nature. Consider carefully before introducing these plants into your landscape. You may find that they outcompete desirable plants and cause you pain in the form of headaches and backaches for years to come.

Aegopodium podagraria

Bishop's goutweed, ground elder,
   Bishop's weed

Family: Apiaceae (Parsley)

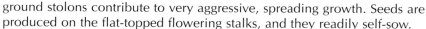

Plant type/description: Bishop's weed is a herbaceous perennial groundcover that spreads indefinitely. Flat-topped flowers characteristic of the parsley family bloom in June. Three (or sometimes seven to nine) leaflets occur on each compound leaf.

Cause for concern: Bishop's weed is tolerant of a wide range of soils, and underground stolons contribute to very aggressive, spreading growth. Seeds are produced on the flat-topped flowering stalks, and they readily self-sow.

Zones: 4–8

Origin: Europe

Lists: STATE, in Connecticut it is banned, and in Vermont it is listed as a Class B noxious weed

Bishop's weed may cause allergic contact dermatitis in sensitive individuals and cause symptoms much like poison oak or poison ivy. Variegated forms are particularly handsome. Deadhead to prevent seed formation, and use only in a restricted root zone area.

Euphorbia cyparissias

Cypress spurge

Family: Euphorbiaceae (Spurge)

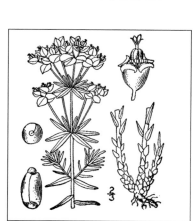

Plant type/description: Cypress spurge is an erect, branching, rhizomatous perennial with linear leaves and yellowish-green flowers. Stems and leaves emit a poisonous milky sap when broken. Plants grow about 12 inches tall and spread indefinitely.

Cause for concern: This invasive perennial

136

reproduces by seed and lateral root buds. It is found in pastures, fields, along fencerows and roadsides, and in landscapes. Seeds are explosively dehiscent, and they are spread by ants. Plants are potentially toxic to horses and cattle.

Zones: 4–8

Origin: Europe

Lists: STATE, WI, noxious weed in Colorado, banned in Connecticut

Keep well away from perennial beds and borders, for it will quickly overtake them. Cypress spurge is found in every state except Nevada, New Mexico, Arizona, Texas, Louisiana, and Mississippi.

Coronilla varia

Crown vetch

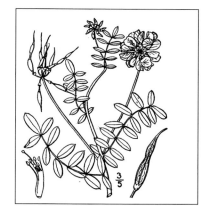

Family: Fabaceae (Pea)

Plant type/description: Crown vetch is an herbaceous perennial legume with creeping stems two to eight feet long. Attractive pinkish-lavender to white flowers bloom in clusters from May to August. Flowers are followed by pealike seedpods.

Cause for concern: Plants spread by seeds and vegetatively by creeping roots which can grow up to ten feet long.

Zones: 3–9

Origin: Europe, Africa, Asia

Lists: SEEPPC, USFWS, WI

Crown vetch has been planted extensively on roadsides, banks, and other areas prone to erosion in many places in the United States. Prescribed burning repeated over a period of several years may be needed to control this species in fire-adapted communities. Repeated mowing may help in its eradication, and foliar herbicides have also proven effective.

Euonymus fortunei

Wintercreeper

Family: Celastraceae (Bittersweet)

Plant type/description: Wintercreeper is a dense, woody-stemmed, evergreen, shrublike vine. Dark green oval-shaped leaves about 1 to 2.5 inches long occur in pairs along the stems. Stems have many trailing roots. Clusters of inconspicuous greenish-white flowers bloom in summer and are followed by pinkish to red capsules that split open and reveal seeds that are covered with a fleshy orange seed coat.

Cause for concern: Wintercreeper can become an ecological threat because of its rapid growth and ability to tolerate diverse conditions. It can displace native vegetation quickly by forming a dense cover either in the canopy or on the floor of a forest. The seeds float readily, so it floats down streams and invades riparian areas. Seeds are attractive to wildlife and birds, which also spread it far and wide.

Zones: 3–9

Origin: China, Japan, Korea

Lists: SEEPPC, USFWS, WI

Wintercreeper may take the form of a trailing groundcover, a mounding shrub, or a climbing vine. The cultivar 'Coloratus' is a popular evergreen groundcover. Use in the Deep South is limited by scale infestations and diseases. Wintercreeper can be purchased at many nurseries and on-line sources.

Houttuynia cordata 'Chameleon'

Chinese lizard tail, variegated fishwort, tricolor heartleaf

Family: Saururaceae (Lizard's-tail)

Plant type/description: Houttuynia is a deciduous groundcover about one foot tall that spreads vigorously by underground rhizomes. Flowers are white but barely noticeable among the more colorful foliage. Leaves are heart shaped and bordered with multicolors of pink, cream, green, and bronze.

Cause for concern: Although I see no evidence that *Houttuynia* has escaped into natural areas, it seems to be a real thug in gardens. Spreading by creeping rhizomes, it overruns desirable perennials. Trying to rid the garden of this weed is a difficult task because any piece of root left behind will produce another plant. Rhizomes become entangled with those of desirable perennials. Plants are tolerant of most herbicides.

Zones: 5–8

Origin: Japan and mountainous regions of eastern Asia

Lists: None

Although this plant has not appeared on lists that I have researched, I have found overwhelming evidence regarding its invasiveness in gardens. Of 19 comments on the website Dave's Garden (http://davesgarden.com), five gave it positive comments, five were neutral, and nine were negative. Most negative comments referred to its invasiveness and included strong suggestions to other gardeners that it should be avoided.

Hypericum perforatum

St. John's wort, Klamath weed

Family: Clusiaceae (Mangosteen)

Plant type/description: St. John's wort is an erect, semiwoody, perennial rhizomatous herb. Attractive clusters of yellow flowers are produced at the tips of branches. Fruit is a capsule with many small, dark, cylindrical seeds.

Cause for concern: St. John's wort reproduces by seeds and spreads by rhizomes. It competes with and replaces native species. Plants have spread to cultivated fields, pastures, and waste areas in many parts of the United States.

Zones: Throughout continental United States

Origin: Europe

Lists: NE&GP, SEEPPC, STATE, WI, WSWS

Like many invasive species, St. John's wort was most likely brought to the United States as an ornamental. It has many medicinal applications. Hypericum has mood-elevating properties and is effective in the treatment of anxiety and sleep disorders, as well as many other ailments that plague humans.

Polygonum cuspidatum syn. *Fallopia japonica*

Japanese knotweed, Mexican bamboo, fleeceflower

Family: Polygonaceae (Buckwheat)

Plant type/description: Japanese knotweed is an herbaceous perennial that reproduces by seeds and by large rhizomes. Stems are hollow and bamboo-like, and attractive sprays of whitish flowers bloom in summer. Flowers are followed by small winged fruits.

Cause for concern: This weed spreads quickly to form dense thickets that exclude native vegetation. It is currently established in 36 states from Maine to Wisconsin and south to Louisiana. It is also scattered in some of the Midwest and western states.

Zones: All zones

Origin: Eastern Asia

Lists: N'EAST, SEEPC, STATE, USFWS, WSWS

Japanese knotweed can flourish under a wide variety of conditions, including full shade, high temperatures, salinity, and drought. Gardeners should also be wary of *Polygonum perfoliatum,* which is commonly called mile-a-minute vine. It is also an invasive species in many parts of the United States.

Vinca major and *Vinca minor*

Periwinkle, myrtle

Family: Apocynaceae (Dogbane)

Plant type/description: Vinca major and *V. minor* are
  evergreen, perennial vines with trailing stems.
  Blue to violet five-petaled flowers bloom in
  spring. Foliage may be solid green or variegated.

Cause for concern: Spread is rapid and indeterminate. Arching stems root where they touch the
  soil. Those who choose to grow this groundcover
  should place it in an area where it is confined by
  solid structures to prevent its spread. Infestations
  occur in natural forest areas, riparian zones, and
  urban areas. Spread is caused by floating vegetation and debris and by
  dumping of garden refuse. Stem fragments root wherever they land.

Zones: 7–9

Origin: Southern Europe

Lists: SEEPPC, WI

Vinca major is larger and more aggressive than *V. minor.* Plants grow in sun
or shade and can quickly cover an area. Both plants are easily obtained at
garden centers and mail-order or on-line sources.

Both vines are attractive trailing over the edges of container plantings.
Care should be exercised, however, even when placing these vines in container plantings because the stems will grow to the ground and then take off
into neighboring beds. Vinca is often seen spreading into natural areas from
old homesites where it was planted years ago. Once established, it grows
into a thick groundcover that overtakes other groundcover herbs. *Vinca
minor* has more tenacious roots than *V. major.*

Groundcovers for Specific Situations

Groundcovers for Sun

Abelia grandiflora (Abelia)

Agapanthus africanus (Lily of the Nile)

Allium tuberosum (Garlic Chives)

Aloe saponaria (Soap Aloe)

Aptenia cordifolia (Baby Sun Rose)

Arachis glabrata (Ornamental Peanut)

Armeria maritima (Sea Thrift)

Artemisia stelleriana (Dusty Miller)

Buxus microphylla (Boxwood)

Bulbine frutescens (Bulbine)

Ceratostigma plumbaginoides (Dwarf Plumbago)

Centella asiatica (Goto Kola)

Conradina canescens (Wild Rosemary)

Coreopsis lanceolata (Lanceleaf Coreopsis)

Cotoneaster horizontalis (Rockspray Cotoneaster)

Cuphea hyssopifolia (Mexican Heather)

Delosperma cooperi (Ice Plant)

Dichondra carolinensis (Dichondra)

Dietes vegeta (African Iris)

Eragrostis spectabilis (Love Grass)

Evolvulus glomeratus (Blue Daze)

Gaillardia pulchella (Blanket Flower)

Gardenia augusta 'Prostrata' (Trailing Gardenia)

Helianthus debilis (Beach Sunflower)

Helichrysum angustifolium (Curry)

Hemerocallis spp. (Daylily)

Ilex spp. (Holly)

Ipomoea pes-caprae (Railroad Vine)

Juniperus spp. (Juniper)

Lantana spp. (Lantana)

Licania michauxii (Gopher Apple)

Muhlenbergia capillaris (Muhly Grass)

Nandina domestica (Nandina)

Origanum spp. (Oregano)

Phlox subulata (Moss Phlox)

Pittosporum tobira 'Wheeleri' (Dwarf Pittosporum)

Mazus reptans (Powderpuff)

Phyla nodiflora (Frogfruit)

Raphiolepis indica (Indian Hawthorne)

Rosmarinus officinalis (Rosemary)

Santolina spp. (Santolina)

Sedum acre (Goldmoss Sedum)

Serenoa repens (Saw Palmetto)

Sisyrinchium angustifolium (Blue-eyed Grass)

Stachys byzantina (Lamb's Ears)

Thymus spp. (Thyme)

Trachelospermum asiaticum (Asiatic Jasmine)

Tradescantia ohiensis (Spiderwort)

Tradescantia pallida (Purple Heart)

Tulbaghia violacea (Society Garlic)

Yucca filamentosa (Bear Grass)

Groundcovers that are Drought Tolerant

Aloe saponaria (Soap Aloe)

Aptenia cordifolia (Baby Sun Rose)

Arachis glabrata (Ornamental Peanut)

Artemisia stelleriana (Dusty Miller)

Bulbine frutescens (Bulbine)

Conradina canescens (Wild Rosemary)

Coreopsis lanceolata (Lanceleaf Coreopsis)

Delosperma cooperi (Ice Plant)

Dietes vegeta (African Iris)

Eragrostis spectabilis (Love Grass)

Evolvulus glomeratus (Blue Daze)

Gaillardia pulchella (Blanket Flower)

Hedera canariensis (Algerian Ivy)

Helianthus debilis (Beach Sunflower)

Helichrysum angustifolium (Curry)

Ipomoea pes-caprae (Railroad Vine)

Juniperus spp. (Juniper)

Lantana spp. (Lantana)

Licania michauxii (Gopher Apple)

Liriope (Liriope)

Muhlenbergia capillaris (Muhly Grass)

Ophiopogon (Mondo Grass)

Origanum spp. (Oregano)

Rosmarinus officinalis (Rosemary)

Phlox subulata (Moss Phlox)

Rubus pentalobus (Creeping Raspberry)

Santolina spp. (Santolina)

Sedum acre (Goldmoss Sedum)

Serenoa repens (Saw Palmetto)

Stachys byzantina (Lamb's Ears)

Thymus spp. (Thyme)

Trachelospermum asiaticum (Asiatic Jasmine)

Tradescantia ohiensis (Spiderwort)

Tradescantia pallida (Purple Heart)

Yucca filamentosa (Bear Grass)

Zamia pumila (Coontie)

Groundcovers for Shade

Adiantum pedatum (Maidenhair Fern)

Ajuga reptans (Ajuga)

Aspidistra elatior (Cast Iron Plant)

Asplenium platyneuron (Ebony Spleenwort)

Astilbe spp. (False spirea)

Athyrium filix-femina (Lady Fern)

Athyrium goeringianum (Japanese Painted Fern)

Bletilla striata (Chinese Ground Orchid)

Calathea louisae (Emerald Feather Calathea)

Cephalotaxus harringtonia (Spreading Yew)

Chrysogonum virginianum (Green and Gold)

Cyrtomium falcatum (Holly Fern)

Danae racemosa (Alexandrian Laurel)

Dennstaedtia punctilobula (Hay-scented Fern)

Dryopteris erythrosora (Autumn Fern)

Dryopteris ludoviciana (Southern Shield Fern)

Epimedium spp. (Barrenwort)

Ficus pumila (Creeping Fig)

Galium odoratum Sweet Woodruff)

Gaultheria procumbens (Teaberry)

Hedera canariensis (Algerian Ivy)

Hexastylis arifolia (Heartleaf Wild Ginger)

Hosta spp. (Hosta)

Lamium maculatum (Spotted Deadnettle)

Liriope spp. (Liriope)

Mitchella repens (Partridgeberry)

Onoclea sensibilis (Sensitive Fern)

Osmunda regalis (Regal Fern)

Pachysandra procumbens (Allegheny Spurge)

Packera aurea (Golden ragwort)

Polystichum polyblepharum (Tassel Fern)

Pulmonaria spp. (Lungwort)

Rumohra adiantiformis (Leatherleaf Fern)

Saxifraga stolonifera (Creeping Raspberry)

Selaginella braunii (Selaginella)

Trachelospermum asiaticum (Asiatic Jasmine)

Waldsteinia ternata (Barren Strawberry)

Groundcovers that are Salt Tolerant (H = High, M = Moderate)

Agapanthus africanus (Lily of the Nile) M

Aloe saponaria (Soap Aloe) H

Armeria maritime (Sea Thrift) H

Aptenia cordifolia (Baby Sun Rose) H

Arachis glabrata (Ornamental Peanut) H

Artemisia stelleriana (Dusty Miller) H

Aspidistra elatior (Cast Iron Plant) M

Bergenia cordifolia (Heartleaf Bergenia) M

Buxus microphylla (Boxwood) M

Ceratostigma plumbaginoides (Dwarf Plumbago) M

Conradina canescens (Wild Rosemary) H

Crinum erubescens (String Lily) M

Cyrtomium falcatum (Holly Fern) M

Delosperma cooperi (Ice Plant) H

Dennstaedtia punctilobula (Hay-scented Fern) H

Dichondra repens carolinensis (Dichondra) H

Evolvulus glomeratus (Blue Daze) H

Ficus pumila (Creeping Fig) H

Gaillardia pulchella (Blanket Flower) H

Hedera canariensis (Algerian Ivy) H

Helianthus debilis (Beach Sunflower) H

Hemerocallis spp. (Daylily) H

Hosta spp. (Hosta) M

Heuchera 'Purple Palace' (Alumroot) M

Ilex crenata (Japanese Holly) M

Ipomoea pes-caprae (Railroad Vine) H

Juniperus spp. (Juniper) H

Lantana spp. (Lantana) H

Licania michauxii (Gopher Apple) H

Liriope spp. (Liriope) M

Mimosa strigillosa (Powderpuff) M

Muhlenbergia capillaris Mully Grass) H

Phyla nodiflora (Frogfruit) H

Pittosporum tobira (Dwarf Pittosporum) H

Raphiolepis indica (Indian Hawthorne) H

Rosmarinus officinalis (Rosemary) H

Rumohra adiantiformis (Leatherleaf Fern) M

Santolina spp. (Santolina) M

Sedum acre (Goldmoss Sedum) H

Serenoa repens (Saw Palmetto) H

Trachelospermum asiaticum (Asiatic Jasmine) M

Tradescantia pallida (Purple Heart) H

Tulbaghia violacea (Society Garlic) M

Yucca filamentosa (Bear Grass) H

Aristida stricta (Wiregrass)

Groundcovers for Wet/Damp Places

Agapanthus africanus (Lily of the Nile)
Centella asiatica (Gotu Kola)
Dietes vegeta (African Iris)
Galium odoratum (Sweet Woodruff)
Gelsemium sempervirens (Carolina Jasmine)
Hedera canariensis (Algerian Ivy)
Onoclea sensibilis (Sensitive Fern)
Osmunda regalis (Royal Fern)
Packera aurea (Golden Ragwort)
Tiarella cordifolia (Foamflower)

Picture Credits

All line drawings in this section are not copyrighted and may be used freely for any purpose.

The following line drawings were taken from:

USDA-NRCS PLANTS Database / Britton, N.L, and A. Brown. 1913. *Illustrated flora of the northern states and Canada.* They were downloaded from USDA, NRCS. 2005. *The PLANTS Database*, Version 3.5 Data compiled from various sources by Mark W. Skinner. Baton Rouge, LA 70874-4490 USA.

    Adiantum pedatum, Vol. 1: 31
    Aegopodium podagraria, Vol. 2: 654
    Armeria maritima, Vol. 2: 718
    Artemisia abrotanum, Vol 3: 526
    Artemisia stelleriana, Vol. 3: 527
    Asplenium platyneuron, Vol. 1: 27
    Centella asiatica, Vol. 2: 651
    Chrysogonum virginianum, Vol. 3: 463
    Coronilla varia, Vol. 2: 392
    Dennstaedtia punctilobula, Vol. 1: 14
    Dichondra carolinensis, Vol. 3: 40
    Euphorbia cyparissias, Vol. 2: 474
    Galium odoratum, Vol. 3: 267
    Gaultheria procumbens, Vol 2: 693
    Heuchera americana var. *hispida,* Vol 2: 227
    Hypericum perforatum, Vol. 2: 533
    Lamium maculatum, Vol. 3: 122
    Mentha x piperita, Vol. 3: 151
    Onoclea sensibilis, Vol. 1: 11
    Osmunda regalis, Vol. 1: 7
    Pachysandra procumbens, Vol. 2: 480

    Packera aurea, Vol. 3: 544
    Phegopteris hexagonoptera, Vol. 1: 23
    Phyla nodiflora, Vol. 3: 98
    Polygonum cuspidatum, Vol. 1: 676
    Polystichum acrostichoides, Vol. 1: 16
    Tiarella cordifolia, Vol. 2: 224
    Vinca major, Vol. 3: 20
    Viola odorata, Vol. 2: 558
    Woodwardia areolata, Vol. 1: 25
    Yucca filamentosa, Vol. 1: 513

The two grasses below were taken from:

USDA-NRCS PLANTS Database / Hitchcock, A.S. (rev. A. Chase). 1950. *Manual of the grasses of the United States.* UADA Misc. Publ. No. 200. Washington, DC. They are not copyrighted and were downloaded from the same source as above.

    Aristida stricta
    Eragrostis spectabilis

Other pictures and illustrations:

Center for Aquatic and invasive Plants, University of Florida, Gainesville. Used with permission:

    Lygodium japnoicum: Line Drawing by Sandra Murphy-Pak
    Nephrolepis cordifolia: Drawing by Ana Ramey
    Salvinia molesta: Line Drawing by Laura Line

Photograph of daylily rust:

    University of Iowa Extension. Photo by Daren Mueller. Used with permission.

Photograph of sooty mold:
University of Florida Extension.
Photo by Theresa Friday. Used
with permission.

Illustrations by Joe Stoy:
Abelia x *grandiflora*
Astilbe spp.
Berberis candidula
Bergenia cordifolia
Buxus microphylla
Danae racemosa
Epimedium spp.
Helichrysum angustifolium
Laurentia fluviatilis
Mazus reptans
Pulmonaria spp.
Serissa foetida

*All photographs by Marie
Harrison (unless otherwise stat-
ed)*

Illustrations by Marie Harrison:
Buxus sempervirens
Cotoneaster horizontalis
Gaultheria procumbens
Heuchera spp.
Ipomoea pes-caprae
Mimosa strigillosa
Stachys byzantina
Euonymus fortunei
Houttuynia cordata
Sarcococca hookeriana var.
humilis

Map on page 16 courtesy of U.S. National Arboretum, USDA-ARS

Bibliography

It would be impossible to list all of the references that I consulted while writing this book. Numerous gardening friends and acquaintances in Florida and in other states in the South have shared their experiences and knowledge. Chat rooms on the internet, numerous websites, books, periodicals, and pamphlets have been useful. However, the books listed below are in my personal gardening library, and they have been some of the most useful references.

Bender, Steve. *The Southern Living Garden Book*. Birmingham, AL: Oxmoor House, 1998.

Bender, Steve and Felder Rushing. *Passalong Plants*. Chapel Hill, NC: UNC Press, 1993.

Black, Robert J. and Edward F. Gilman. *Landscape Plants for the Gulf and South Atlantic Coasts, Selection, Establishment, and Maintenance*. Gainesville, FL: University Press of Florida, 2004.

Chaplin, Lois Trigg and Monica Moran Brandies. *The Florida Gardener's Book of Lists*. Dallas, TX: Taylor Publishing, 1998.

Dirr, Michael A. *Manual of Woody Landscape Plants, Their Identification, Ornamental Characteristics, Culture, Propagation, and Uses*. Champaign, IL: Stipes Publishing, 1990.

Hill, Madalene and Gwen Barclay, with Jean Hardy. *Southern Herb Growing*. Fredericksburg, TX: Shearer Publishing, 1987.

Lower, Peter. *Ornamental Grasses for the Southeast*. Nashville, TN. Cool Springs Press, 2003.

Mickel, John T. *Ferns for American Gardens*. Portland, OR: Timber Press, 2003.

Nelson, Gil. *The Ferns of Florida*. Sarasota, Florida: Pineapple Press, 2000.

Ogden, Scott. *Garden Bulbs for the South*. Dallas, TX: Taylor Publishing, 1994.

Osorio, Rufino. *A Gardener's Guide to Florida's Native Plants*. Gainesville, FL: University Press of Florida, 2001.

Rushing, Felder. *Tough Plants for Southern Gardens, Low Care, No Care, Tried and True Winners*. Nashville, TN: Cool Springs Press, 2003.

Seidenberg, Charlotte. *The Wildlife Garden, Planning Backyard Habitats*. Jackson, MS: University Press of Mississippi, 1995.

Sullivan, Barbara J. *Garden Perennials for the Coastal South*. Chapel Hill, NC: University Press of North Carolina, 2003.

USDA-NRCS. 2005. **The PLANTS Database** (http://plants.usda.gov). National Plant Data Center, Baton Rouge, LA 70874-4490 USA.

Wasowski, Sally with Andy Wasowski. *Gardening with Native Plants of the South*. Dallas, TX: Taylor Publishing, 1994.

Welch, Dr. William. *Perennial Garden Color: Perennials, Cottage Gardens, Old Roses, and Companion Plants.* Dallas, TX: Taylor Publishing, 1989.

Winter, Norman. *Tough-as-Nails Flowers for the South.* Jackson, MS: University Press of Mississippi, 2003.

Websites and Publications from Cooperative Extension Services

Auburn University and Alabama A&M University, www.aces.edu/

Clemson University, Clemson, South Carolina, www.clemson.edu/extension/

Louisiana State University, www.agctr.lsu.edu/

Mississippi State University, www.msucares.com/

North Carolina State University and NC A&T University, www.ces.ncsu.edu/

Oklahoma State University, http://pods.dasnr.okstate.edu/

Texas A&M University, http://texasextension.tamu.edu/

University of Arkansas. www.uaex.edu/

University of Florida, http://edis.ifas.ufl.edu/

University of Georgia, www.ces.uga.edu/

Index

Hypericum perforatum, 139

ice plant, 21, 31
Ilex crenata 'Border Gem', 59
immortelle, 134
incised halberd fern, 121
Indian blanket, 15, 71
Indian hawthorn, 66
Ipomoea pes-caprae, 128
Iridaceae, 32, 81
iris family, 32, 81
iron fern, 54
iron plant, 23
ivy, 99

Japanese barberry, 123
Japanese climbing fern, 121
Japanese holly, 59
Japanese holly fern, 51
Japanese honeysuckle, 9, 100
Japanese knotweed, 139
Japanese lace fern, 53
Japanese mock orange, 65
Japanese painted fern, 117
Japanese red shield fern, 52
Japanese sedge, 27
Japanese shore juniper, 61
Japanese spurge, 129
Japanese tassel fern, 53
Japanese wood fern, 52
Juniperus chinensis var. *sargentii*, 60
Juniperus conferta, 61
Juniperus horizontalis, 74

kidney grass, 127
Klamath weed, 139
Korean tassel fern, 53

lady fern, 50

lamb's ears, 135
Lamiaceae, 19, 69, 88, 89, 90, 92, 93, 94, 98, 112, 134, 135
Lamium maculatum, 112
Lampranthus, 21
lanceleaf coreopsis, 70
landscape fabrics, 12
Lantana camara, 13, 62
Lantana montevidensis, 63
latherwort, 102
Laurentia fluviatilis, 113
lavender cotton, 91
leadwort, 28
leadwort family, 28, 109
leatherleaf fern, 54
Licania michauxii, 75
Liliaceae, 20, 23, 25, 36, 38, 39, 40, 41, 48, 122, 125
lily family, 20, 23, 25, 36, 38, 39, 40, 41, 48, 122, 125
lily of the Nile, 18
lilyturf, 39, 41
Liriope muscari, 39
Liriope spicata, 40
little brown jug, 73
little-leaf jasmine, 46
littleleaf box, 124
lobelia family, 113
Lobeliaceae, 113
Lonicera japonica, 9, 100
loosestrife family, 30
lungwort, 114
Lygodiaceae, 121
Lygodium japonicum, 121
Lygodium microphyllum, 121
Lysimachia nummularia, 101
Lythraceae, 30

madder family, 57, 76, 115, 133
maidenhair fern, 116

Singapore daisy, 103
Sisyrinchium angustifolium, 81
snake flower, 25
snakebeard, 41
snotweed, 83
snow rose, 115
soap aloe, 20
soapwort, 102
society garlic, 95
Southern lady fern, 50
Southern shield fern, 117, 120
southernwood, 132
spearmint, 134
Sphagneticola trilobata, 103
spice berry, 111
spiderwort, 83
spiderwort family, 47, 83
spikemoss family, 45
spleenwort family, 116
spotted deadnettle, 112
spurge family, 136
squaw vine, 76
squawberry, 76
St. John's wort, 139
Stachys byzantina, 135
Stoke's aster, 82
Stokesia laevis, 82
stonecrop, 44
stonecrop family, 44
stout blue-eyed grass, 81
strawberry begonia, 43
strawberry geranium, 43
string lily, 29
sweet box, 114
sweet myrtle, 87
sweet violet, 135
sweet woodruff, 133
sweet-scented bedstraw, 133
sword fern, 121

tarragon, 132
tassel fern, 53
teaberry, 111
Tectaria incisa, 121
Teucrium chamaedrys, 93
Thelypteridaceae, 119, 120
Thelypteris kunthii, 120
thrift, 79
Thymus praecox, 94
Thymus serpyllum, 94
Tiarella cordifolia, 130
tickseed, 70
toad lily, 48
Trachelospermum asiaticum, 46
Trachelospermum jasminoides, 46
Tradescantia ohiensis, 83
Tradescantia pallida 'Purpurea', 47
trailing daisy, 103
trailing gardenia, 57
trailing ice plant, 31
trailing juniper, 74
trailing lantana, 63
trailing rosemary, 90
tricolor heartleaf, 138
Tricyrtis hirta, 48
Tricyrtis spp., 48
Tulbaghia violacea, 95
turkey-tangle fogfruit (or frogfruit), 130

urn orchid, 24

variegated fishwort, 138
variegated Japanese sedge, 27
verbena family, 62, 63
Verbenaceae, 62, 63
Veronica peduncularis 'Georgia Blue', 108

Here are some other books from Pineapple Press on related topics. For a complete catalog, write to Pineapple Press, P.O. Box 3889, Sarasota, Florida 34230-3889, or call (800) 746-3275. Or visit our website at www.pineapplepress.com.

Southern Gardening: An Environmentally Sensitive Approach by Marie Harrison. A comprehensive guide to beautiful, environmentally conscious yards and gardens. Suggests useful groundcovers and easy-care, adaptable trees, shrubs, perennials, and annuals. A month-by-month guide helps gardeners plan ahead as they strive to have earth-friendly gardens. (pb)

Gardening in the Coastal South by Marie Harrison. A Master Gardener discusses coastal gardening considerations such as salt tolerance; environmental issues such as pesticide use, beneficial insects, and exotic invasives; and specific issues such as gardening for butterflies and birds. Color photos and charming pen-and-ink illustrations round out the text, which covers perennials, herbs, shrubs and small trees, vines, and edible flowers. (pb)

The Art of South Florida Gardening by Harold Songdahl and Coralee Leon. Gardening advice specifically written for the unique conditions of south Florida. This practical, comprehensive guide, written with humor and know-how, will teach you how to outsmart the soil, protect against pests and weather, and select the right trees and shrubs for Florida's climate. (pb)

Exotic Foods: A Kitchen and Garden Guide by Marian Van Atta. Take advantage of year-round warm weather and grow fruit trees, exotic vegetables, and rare delights such as Surinam cherry. Discover tips to keep your garden free of pests and producing for years. Includes a wealth of delicious and nutritious recipes for drinks, main courses, desserts, relishes, jams, and jellies. (pb)

Flowering Trees of Florida by Mark Stebbins. If you just can't get enough of majestic trees, brightly colored flowers, and anything that grows from the ground up, you'll love this book. Written for both the seasoned arborist and the weekend gardener alike, this comprehensive guide offers 74 outstanding tropical flowering trees that will grow in Florida's subtropical climate. Full-color photos throughout. (pb)

The Ferns of Florida by Gil Nelson. The first field guide in 25 years to treat Florida's amazing variety of ferns. Includes color plates with more than 200 images, notes on each species' growth form and habit, general remarks about its botanical and common names, unique characteristics, garden use, and history in Florida. (hb & pb)

Guide to the Gardens of Florida by Lilly Pinkas. This comprehensive guide to Florida's gardens includes detailed information about featured species and garden facilities as well as directions, hours of operation, and admission fees. Learn the history and unique offerings of each garden, what plants to see and the best time of year to see them. Traveling outside of Florida? Check out *Guide to the Gardens of Georgia* and *Guide to the Gardens of South Carolina* by the same author. (pb)

Landscaping in Florida by Mac Perry. A photo idea book packed with irresistible ideas for inviting entryways, patios, pools, walkways, and more. Over 200 photos and eight pages of color photos, plus charts of plant materials by region, condition of soil and sunlight, and purpose. (pb)

The Mongo Mango Cookbook by Cynthia Thuma. Much more than a book of easy-to-make recipes, The Mongo Mango Cookbook is also a compendium of mango history, legend, literature, and lore. It traces the fragrant fruit's genesis and its proliferation throughout the world's warm climates. It also explains why the mango's versatility and palate-pleasing flavor make it a favorite among the world's most creative chefs. Extensive appendices include lists of current cultivars and mango-growing countries as well as information on nurseries and garden clubs around Florida. (pb)

Ornamental Tropical Shrubs by Amanda Jarrett. Stunning color photos and full information profile for 83 shrubs including country of origin, drought and salt tolerance, growth rate and suitable soils, preferred sun exposure, mature size and form, flowers and fruits, potential insect and disease problems, and more. (hb & pb)

Poisonous Plants and Animals of Florida and the Caribbean by David W. Nellis. An illustrated guide to the characteristics, symptoms, and treatments for over 300 species of poisonous plants and toxic animals. (hb)

Priceless Florida by Ellie Whitney, Bruce Means, and Anne Rudloe. An extensive, full-color guide to the incomparable ecological riches of this unique region in a way that will appeal to young and old, laypersons and scientists. A cornucopia of colorful illustrations and exquisite photos makes you feel you're there. The comprehensive text enlightens with facts and brims with intriguing curiosities while bridging multiple fields in a crisp, readable style. (hb & pb)

Seashore Plants of South Florida and the Caribbean by David W. Nellis. A full-color guide to the flora of nearshore environments, including complete characteristics of each plant as well as ornamental, medicinal, ecological, and other aspects. Suitable for backyard gardeners and serious naturalists. (pb)

The Trees of Florida by Gil Nelson. The first comprehensive guide to Florida's amazing variety of tree species, this book serves as both a reference and a field guide. (hb & pb)